M000092333

THE BATTLE OF THE BULGE

Brothers
Behind Enemy Lines

by
Suzanne Agnes

Copyright © 2018 by Suzanne Agnes

All rights reserved.

No part of this publication may be reproduced, stored in a retrieval system,
or transmitted in any form or by any means—electronic, mechanical, photocopy-
ing, recording, or otherwise without the prior written permission of the publisher.

ISBN: 978-0-938075-99-8

Printed in the United States of America
22 21 20 19 18 5 4 3 2 1

For Joan Elizabeth,
My beloved mother and my sons' wonderful Grandma Joan
Joan walked her life with grace and love.

CONTENTS

PREFACE

After my beloved mother, Joan, passed, I spent over a decade talking with my dad, George, about his life with my mother. Our conversations were a way for my dad and me to have a connection, to talk about how he and my mother built a happy life together, despite their losses. Our talks helped my dad to appreciate the sweetness of his life. It helped him fight off his sorrow by giving us a project to work on together. It also gave me a project to work on that we knew would not be completed until after he passed—his gift to me for the future, to find happiness after he was gone. The following is a distillation of our ten-year conversation, an exploration of our family ties and love.

In 1944, George Zak, a 19-year-old United States Army private first class, was captured on the front line during the largest and one of the deadliest battles of World War II in Europe. U.S. soldiers defended a seventy-mile stretch of forest in western Europe in bitter winter conditions. Unknown to the U.S. forces, a desperate Hitler launched a massive attack, which resulted in the deaths of more than nineteen thousand American soldiers. This massacre is called the Battle of the Bulge.

George, forced to work as a slave laborer following his capture, subsequently escaped from two different prisoner-of-war camps. German captors abandoned their prisoners before the onslaught of the Russian Army. George was free to go. However, Russian cossacks on horseback recaptured George minutes after he found out he was free to leave German captivity.

Inside American-held territory, George's brother, Robert, a U.S. Army radioman, was determined to find where George might be held prisoner. Robert took his jeep and led his own personal rescue mission into enemy territory to find George. At the same time, George engineered his own escape and led a group of prisoners away from Russian captivity. Miraculously, the Zak brothers met on the road in enemy territory (then eastern Germany) while searching for each other. Together, they now had to escape through Russian lines and into American-held territory.

Instead of immediately returning to freedom in the safety of American-held territory, however, the Zak brothers decided to stay and rescue even more American soldiers. Fearing that the Russians might recognize George as an escaped prisoner, Robert disguised his emaciated brother with his helmet and gave George his rifle to carry. In order to avoid Russian capture, Robert, George, and the other rescued Americans decided to look like an army. The Zak brothers lined up their compatriots and determined to do whatever it would take to lead all of them to freedom.

⎯

I grew up in 1970's Chicagoland. My parents often told me that they had a "mixed marriage," referring to their Irish and Bohemian heritages, which I thought was ridiculous. I was a vision of 1970's fashion. I wore my hair hot-pressed back into a wind tunnel glued down with aqua net. I wore striped socks, yellow corduroy elephant pants, pot-holder crocheted, red, white, and blue vests and, of course, gold octagon granny glasses. I listened to "Billy,

Don't Be a Hero, Don't Be a Fool with Life" by Paper Lace. My dad informed me that this was the worst song he had ever heard. I countered with,

"Well if you were a prisoner of war, why is your favorite show 'Hogan's Heroes'?"

Indeed, George's favorite television show was "Hogan's Heroes"; it made him roar with laughter. With a blaring laugh track, "Hogan's Heroes" was a comedy of World War II Allied prisoners conducting espionage while being held captive by the German Army.

Colonel Klink.

"You dumbkoff!"

A monocle.

Tricky cute French guy with a beret and a gigantic hidden radio.

Girls! Champagne! Parties. A secret trap door. The good guys win. Motorcycles with sidecars. German helmets with spikes. Long, heavy, woolen army coats.

"Nothing! I know Nothing!" was Klink's catch phrase.

Me, snarky twelve-year-old girl says,

"So Dad, is that how it was in the war? Dad, what is with that stupid show? It's the worst show. I thought you were an American prisoner of war in World War II. How can you watch it?"

Extra snark applied on that delivery. Snark ignored. Instead, he replied,

"I almost got killed many, many times when I was nineteen years old and in combat. Many of my friends were killed right in front of me. We were ordered to surrender. Our commander ordered us to surrender. We broke up our guns. My captain was blown up. I lay on the ground and when a mortar hit, I was thrown up into the air. I was captured and put on a train with hundreds of American GIs. The British started bombing the train yard. And so you get to decide what's on TV?

"I just had those pipe dreams when I was a prisoner of war, and I was wondering, would I live through the day? Men got shot all the time. In camp I used to dream I'd pull pranks on my guards and have laughs, and now I am watching it on 'Hogan's Heroes.' You gotta have fun every day.

"You know, I used to hear sirens in the suburbs at night and think it's bombs. Except they didn't call it PTSD back then; they called it 'battle fatigue.' That must be a new name for an age-old thing. Now I just think 'Hogan's Heroes' is a funny show. It makes me laugh. It's healing."

"Yeah well. I just want you to know that it's unfair around here that you're always hoggin' the TV. The 'Bay City Rollers' special is on TV at seven. S-A-T-U-R-D-A-Y N-I-G-H-T. Why can't I watch what I wanna watch?"

"It's my TV. I paid for it."

"Your point being?"

After I finished college in the 1980s, I worked and traveled around Europe. My father asked me to visit the Belgian battlefield where he was captured. I drove through the gravesites of the soldiers of the Battle of the Bulge. I drove through, and all I could see was hundreds and then thousands of grave markers. I started thinking, "These are not just American boys; these are German boys too, and many were just nineteen years old—younger than me!" The immensity of the slaughter was a dark and depressing experience, and it just went on and on. It was horrible. All those graves for as far as I could drive.

The gloom and despair gripped me. The suffering. Countless graves of dead young men. German and American. All very young and dead in a cruel war. It was quite a shock to see that. Americans and Germans. (These are not just American boys but German boys too. Dead. They were nineteen years old. Like you were, I thought of my dad.) Exactly. The mortal remains of all . . . caught up in this awful, awful war. And that was just one battle. There were plenty more.

"I was allowed to go to a full future," my dad reflected. "I married a wonderful woman. Raised four wonderful children. Had a wonderful job. I was very happy with my life, which I felt was a real gift after being almost killed in so many ways. Not only that day, which I was trying to describe, but for months after that I was almost always being almost killed, which I'll go on to afterward, if there is plenty of time."

(There's plenty of time. Let's begin. George can tell his story.)

—*Suzanne Agnes*

FAMILY
BACKGROUND

My great–grandfather, Gregor Zak, was drafted into Franz Joseph's Austrian Army, where he served for more than fourteen years. When he was released, he took his wife, Anna Fleischmann, and young son, Johan, on the next passenger ship to America. My grandfather Johan was renamed John upon his arrival in America. Gregor and John settled and opened a tailor shop in Chicago's Pilsen neighborhood on the lower west side.

The Zak family bought a house directly across from Mrs. O'Leary, whose infamous cow reputedly started the Great Chicago Fire in 1871 by kicking over a lantern while being milked. The Zaks actually bought their milk from her. 1870's Chicago was built of almost all wooden buildings except for, of course, the limestone Water Tower building, which is still standing on downtown's "Magnificent Mile." Lucky for our family, the fire started across the street and spread north toward the city's downtown, burning not our house but everything in its path for four miles straight to Lake Michigan. Nearly all of the survivors of the fire, including our family, literally stood in Lake Michigan for four days while the city burned to the ground.

The Zak's tailor shop on Zion Street, which later became 18th Place.

I remember going to my grandfather John's house in Pilsen as a child. He had a pool table set up for entertainment for the young people. Grandfather John was a quiet man and a real observer of us. John and his wife, Mary Brom, had taken over the tailor shop from his father.

My mother, Agnes Cervany, was born in 1895 in Chicago in what is now the Cabrini Green neighborhood. She was born of poor working-class parents. Her father was James and her mother was Anna Cervany. James made his living by working with a horse in an open wagon as sort of a delivery man. He would scratch out a living by hauling junk from point A to point B for somebody. To make even a few dollars, he had to work twelve hours a day just to support himself and his two girls, Agnes and Mary.

It was very tough. Mary was ill a lot of the time. It was hard for my mother to see her sister not well, and there was virtually no money for medicine or treatment of any kind. Her father couldn't make much money with his horse and wagon, but he did the best he could. Agnes was always helping in her own little way, but Mary's being sick made it tough for her to have a happy time as a young child. Mary died and then Agnes's mother died, leaving twelve-year-old Agnes as a semi–orphan, with just her father to care for her. Eventually, James could no longer take care of Agnes, so he dropped her off at the Bohemian Aid Society for orphans. This was very painful for my mother, and she only briefly told of her hard times in childhood.

The orphans were shipped out to work for their room and board at various workhouses. Agnes injured her eye as a young lady, working as a seamstress in a horrible accident in a workhouse. She worked at a dress factory, sewing and cutting the cloth. The lady sitting in the chair next to her had a pair of scissors in her hand, and she swung around to talk to somebody and the point of the scissors went into Agnes's eye. It was a miracle that an infection didn't kill her in that day and age.

My mother's poor vision crippled her all her life, and she had a great deal of pain because of the accident. It was so sad, but she never complained about it.

An arrangement was made so she was sent to live with another family as a housekeeper since she couldn't do needlework anymore. Agnes worked as a live-in house maid. Do the laundry, do all the dishes, all the housecleaning, all for her room and board. She had very little money over the years, just what little was doled out to her once in a while. But still she was a happy young lady. Agnes went on to build a happy life for herself despite her abandonment as a young girl. She just had a buoyant attitude.

When Agnes was seventeen, she was living in a particular home where the family had a young son. The young son tried to have a romance with Agnes, but she didn't like the kid at all. The son made real trouble for her. He was constantly trying to get her to out with him and made it really miserable for her. He was really angry, and that went on for a long time. Because he was the son of her employer, there wasn't much she could do about it. The son threatened Agnes that if she ever got married, he would throw acid in her face.

Agnes's future husband, my father, George Zak, was living in the same general neighborhood in Chicago, the Bohemian Pilsen neighborhood. When Agnes was a teenager, she went to school with him. They had gone to a couple of schools together. The Bohemian Pilsen neighborhood hosted several ethnic schools, including the German school and the Bohemian school. George and Agnes attended each of these schools, so they learned German as well as Bohemian, which was their ethnic heritage. Father was a little older than she was, so they weren't in the same classroom. but they were acquainted with each other.

The Bohemian school took all the young people out to Brookfield, a suburb of Chicago, for a picnic. Agnes and George met, and they were quickly attracted to each other as young teenagers. They were good friends and they fell in love.

By this time, the parish priest had gotten Agnes away from the abusive family and found her work with the wealthy McCormack family. She really enjoyed this family, and they were very good to her. She learned how to play the piano.

She told me one time that she took about six or seven of her employer's children to the nearby store. (Agnes spoke several languages: German, English, Bohemian, and another Slovak dialect.) The storekeepers were mocking Agnes for being a young immigrant mother with too many children, but they didn't realize she was fluent in their language. She just pretended that she didn't understand. People are cruel that way to a young girl.

Meanwhile Father was learning engineering at a college. He had joined the National Guard out of patriotism, and World War I was on the horizon. He was a smart man. When the war started, the Illi-

George Zak in uniform as a combat engineer. On the back of the larger photo, he wrote, "Just how I felt the first day after the long sleep. It seems it has not done me much good."

nois National Guard was nationalized into the United States Army, and in due course George went to Texas for basic training and became a combat engineer.

My father and his future wife, Agnes, corresponded with each other for the four years he was fighting in the war. They were really in love, and they felt that they were going to be married when he got back from service.

Mrs. McCormack, Agnes's employer, suddenly died, leaving Agnes homeless once again. The family was broken up, and there was no place for Agnes. The McCormack family gave Mother their family piano as a present.

Her boyfriend, my future father, was now training in Texas for the military. George wrote a letter to his parents to inform them that his girlfriend Agnes was made homeless, she would be moving in to the Zak family home, and they were to treat her as their daughter until he returned and married her. My father wrote that she would sit at his seat at the table and eat his dinner until his return.

Agnes waiting for her soldier fiancé to come home from World War I.

My father thus arranged for Agnes to live with his parents and his ten brothers and sisters for the duration of his time away in Europe, which was four years in combat in the most dangerous position of the army: a combat engineer.

This arrangement turned out to be really wonderful for Agnes. She finally was in a loving situation. My father's parents knew that she was one day going to be their daughter-in-law so it was really sweet of them to take her in.

My father, George Anthony Zak, was a man with wide interests and very patriotic, which had led him to join the Illinois National Guard before World War I started. The army found that they had a true leader in my father. He was offered a commission as a second lieutenant, but my father turned it down. He said that he would feel more at home with the regular guys than he would being an officer. The army accepted that, and my father was designated what we would call today a staff sergeant in charge of forty men as a platoon leader.

He was in one of the first United States Army ships to arrive in France to assist the British, who had their hands full with the Germans. The Germans were threatening to invade Paris. It was static trench warfare in World War I, with Americans and British facing off the Germans mainly in France and Belgium.

In 1918, the British were planning a major attack through the German lines at what they thought was a relatively weak spot. My father's platoon was given a task: in the dark of night, let the British troops come through unnoticed by the Germans.

My father and the men of his division worked hard to learn how to quickly build little bridges over creeks and dig up anti-personnel mines, which they could easily explode in the process. The mine clearing was especially dangerous. His platoon did all kinds of construction work. They worked with the infantry when they could to open up a pathway through difficult terrain for the British cavalry attacks.

My father's platoon was ordered to build a secret bridge over a creek just behind the enemy lines to allow passage of wagons and artillery pieces during the night. They did all of their construction at night because during the day the German aircraft flying overhead would shoot at them.

To hide the construction, the platoon built an undetectable, portable, underwater bridge. They made foundation pillars so they were about three feet below the water line and couldn't be seen from the air. They would cut and shape trees to the appropriate size, driving them into the creek bed until they were actually below the water, and then saw off the tops to be level as a support for the bridge. They built the bridge out of logs that could be assembled and disassembled with bolts.

When it was dark, the platoon would haul the removable and portable bridge slats and put them on top of the pillars. It worked out beautifully. The bridge itself was above the waterline, just high enough to clear the water. The bridge was up all night, then disassembled and hidden before dawn.

The platoon sheltered in the daytime in a bombed-out building; then the next night, they would haul the stuff out and set it up again. The bridge was vital for attacking the Germans. Wagons were hauled over it, food, weapons and ammunition, and soldiers pouring through, all regathering on the other side, providing an improved vantage point from which to attack the enemy. It was really amazing and very clever. Just like my father.

The Germans never really caught on to what my father and his fellow soldiers were doing on an elevated spot by the creek, but they suspected that something was afoot. The Germans finally set up a machine gun nest on a high area over the general area of the creek, and when my father's men would go out in the daytime to check on things or retrieve bolts, the machine gun would open up and start shooting at them.

It was obviously very dangerous for the Americans to be anywhere near the creek during the day. At night, the men were quiet and never lit fires or lights, so the enemy had nothing to shoot at.

Still, that harassing fire kept them from being as efficient as they might have been. Every time the Germans sensed that there was some movement down there, even if they couldn't quite see what it was, they started shooting.

My father and his platoon worked in the secrecy and quiet of night digging out land mines with little shovels or their hands to clear the road. They worked all night long clearing a twenty-foot-wide path of mines. They then marked the side so you could go along the path without stepping on a mine. Just before dawn, they finished and hid in the countryside. My father and his men were told to stand clear and, at dawn, they heard the thunder of hooves coming in their direction.

A thousand British cavalry on horseback galloped through the path my father's men had made and enabled them to get through the weak German line. The British cavalry scattered to the left and the right, flushing the Germans from the rear and causing chaos. The British killed or captured virtually all of the Germans in that whole area.

The British were on horseback with swords and rifles. They made a very stirring sight—an epic movie scene. J.R.R. Tolkien, the author of *The Lord of the Rings,* was in that very same battle, along with my father. Those *Lord of the Rings* battle scenes were based on the slaughter and chaos of the battles of World War I.

My father and his men were awestruck watching the smartly dressed British soldiers in full gallop coming through this road just made for them. It was a big success. The British did a lot of damage behind the German lines by surrounding the German soldiers and overwhelming them with a tough attack.

Now I'm going to skip to maybe ten years after my father was home and safe and married, and he had gone to a luncheon with his wife, Agnes, my mother. They were at a German-American luncheon in Chicago, and George found himself talking to a young man with a German accent. It turned out that this man had been a soldier in the German Army, and Father and this guy swapped stories about what it had been like in their respective armies.

The German started talking about setting up a machine gun nest somewhere, and my father's ears pricked up. He said,

"Was it at such and such a location?"

The guy says,

"Yeah. We were trying to harass these Americans who were possibly building a bridge down there. We wanted to be sure they never did." My father said,

"You've got to be kidding. I was one of those Americans down there that you were shooting at!"

The two men were stunned. These two, once at war against each other, now were peacefully discussing an actual incident in which each had been trying to kill the other. They got to laughing. It was a great and peaceful end of that particular story. They parted on very good terms with no animosity on either's part.

My father was a tough guy, and he was strong and a good leader. He cared for his men. Most of his soldiers survived the war. When World War I was over and peace declared, Father and his men were waiting for orders to be shipped home. They ended up becoming a sort of occupation force simply waiting around all day for orders.

They were very relieved that the Germans had surrendered. They were all going to go home in triumph. However, soon my father noticed that the food ration offered to the enlisted men and himself was not adequate. They were all really hungry all the time. He also noted that the officers were now quartered in a big mansion of some sort and were being fed nice dinners on porcelain plates and had plenty of food in contrast to the enlisted men.

George got his dander up over this, and he finally confronted his captain. He told him about the plight of his men.

"We aren't getting anything to eat and I notice that the officers are feasting on plenty and it's not fair." The officer essentially ignored him and said,

"You are exaggerating, Zak," and he went on his way.

George later found an opportunity to talk to the captain, and this time my father was getting his feathers up and riled over the captain's indifference to the men's plight. Again the captain showed no interest in what my father had to say, and my father got increasingly incensed and belligerent, and he really got angry talking with this officer. Father gave the officer a good shove in the chest.

"You've got to do something about this!"

A yelling match ensued. Finally things calmed down when some other people came along to break it all up. The upshot was that Father was demoted from staff sergeant to private, and he was left behind when all the other soldiers were shipped back home. He had to spend a couple more months in Europe attached to another group as his punishment for manhandling the captain.

George could have faced a court martial and been sentenced to Leavenworth Prison for twenty years, but the officer and his superiors were anxious to get home, and this dustup was a minor irritation to them. My father endured all but was still proud of what he had done. He'd stood up for his men and he had taken the punishment.

My father's job while he was waiting to go home was sitting at a cliff's edge with boxes of hand grenades. He had to pull the pin and throw the hand grenade over the hill to let it explode down below. He didn't mind. He knew that he had done the right thing for his men. He finally came home with another outfit. He returned home a proud man and a hero.

Father survived a lot of combat, and risked his life many times. He saw a lot of death, and he had some amazing stories to tell. When he did come back, he and Agnes were married in September of 1919. My father stationed all of his brothers to act as bodyguards for Agnes during their wedding, just in case the man who had threatened Agnes appeared, but he never did.

After the war ended, they had an apartment and he had a job and was transferred to Detroit, Michigan. They managed to find room and board in a family home. They had their own room, and the people were very nice to them. The husband was the chauffeur and bodyguard for the Henry Ford family.

They were there for about a year, and their first–born, Teresa, my sister was born there. Eventually, they were transferred back to Chicago, and Father spent his career as an engineer with the RC Weibolds Company.

My mother was such a sweetheart and so dedicated to her family and my father. They had a loving marriage and eventually there were more children, all six of us: Teresa, Robert, Margaret, me, Marie, and Tom. Each were born two years apart and each time alternated between a boy and a girl. They planned that very well.

My parents were looking to buy a house, in the suburbs if they could. They wanted to get away from the grim existence of the Pilsen area at the time. Father got on the "L," or elevated train, which ran all the way from the suburbs to downtown Chicago and around a loop that goes all the way around the downtown. Father happened to get on the Garfield Park train that ran all the way due west from Chicago, and he was looking for a nice community out the train window. When he came to Harlem Avenue, which is 7200 West, he saw a church spire coming out of a big building, and he figured that it must be a Catholic church. He and Agnes were very devout Catholics. He got off the train at Harlem Avenue, and sure enough there was St. Bernadine's Catholic Church.

In those days, the church was the main floor of a two-story building. The second floor was a school with twenty-foot ceilings. It was a rugged kind of a building. About half a block away, George saw a For Sale sign on a house on Elgin Avenue. They bought this small bungalow on Elgin Avenue in Forest Park, and they continued to raise their kids in the suburb of Forest Park.

Mother had a wonderful life as an adult, a classic wonderful life. She had many friends in the church. She was a member of the Altar and Rosary Society, a very popular social club for women. Some of the women laundered the special "fair linens" that were used for Mass and the surplices, a lacy sort of over-blouse worn by the priests and altar boys for the religious services.

Mother was always a part of the card parties and social events. She had a lot of friends. People liked her and she liked people. I remember one day hearing her girlfriends gossiping about how awful one fellow parishioner was. My mother ended the discussion by announcing, "He always had the cleanest glasses." That just showed the kind of classy lady that she was. Her credo was "Let's not join in and kick someone when they are down."

When I was a little boy, Father used to take me with him to visit the abandoned and broken soldiers from World War I. Some were blind. Limbless. My father and I regularly went to visit these poor souls in an army retirement home.

My parents were full of great piety and religious feeling. My father was very active for years as a member and president of the Holy Name Society. During the Great Depression, Father helped deliver buckets of coal and food to starving neighbors. He helped people who had less than he did.

He had a job as a structural engineer for years and had a major project of building hospitals and other significant buildings, including some on the Northwestern University campus. He founded and became president of the St. Vincent de Paul Society at our church.

He was also dedicated to encouraging young men to find vocations in the priesthood. He was a very, very busy man; he loved it all and had great satisfaction. He was multitalented and driven. He loved his wife and children and was a good example to us all.

What a great man he was! I was so proud of my father. He was such a well-rounded, good man during both war and peace. He loved a good joke but always clean jokes. He was not a profane man. He was religious and devout and tried to raise his kids that way. Mother was too. Father was a real true leader.

BOYHOOD

When I was a little boy, my parents used to give us all little chores to do around the house: dust the furniture according to our age and abilities. My first job responsibility was as a baker's assistant. My dear mother Agnes always baked three or four loaves of Bohemian rye bread every Saturday, and then we'd have it for Saturday and Sunday dinner. It was delicious. I always had it with grape jelly. It would melt in your mouth.

Mother was busy on this one Saturday. She had this dough in a big bowl and then put it on the top of stove to rise. She said, "George, you are responsible." I was home alone. My job was to make sure that the rising dough didn't spill over the side of the big bowl and run all over the top of the oven.

I said, "Okay, Mom don't worry about it." Off she went, and I promptly forgot about it. Maybe an hour or so later I walked into the kitchen, and I discovered that the oven itself was hot and the darn dough had spilled over and was running over the side of the oven and was baking on the side of the hot oven. Just then as I was looking at this all aghast, the door opened and in came my mother back from her errands. I don't remember (perhaps mercifully) what happened after that.

My mother Agnes had this beautiful, flowing auburn hair all the way down to her shoulders. One day I saw her sitting on her bed combing her hair. She liked to comb it with a brush, brushing her hair and all after Father had gone off to work.

One day she said,

"George. I'm a little tired. Here's a brush and here's how you do it." I was kind of proud. She said,

"I'm going to pay you a penny, you are doing a good job."

We lived a block away from the church, and the lower part of the building was the social area. It had a gym where you could play basketball. The ceiling was somewhat low, but it was good enough for grammar school basketball, and it had a stage on the other end and a lot of folding chairs and places they could hold class plays.

In the evenings, adult classes would be held there or meetings. It was a nice place to be. The folks played cards, bridge, or whatever happened. Mother had a lot of friends at the church was very happy with her life. She would bake for bake sales. I remember she had one friend who had a car and would take her shopping.

Father and Mother never owned their own car. It was the Depression and they couldn't afford it. Neither of them even learned how to drive a car. When my brother Bob turned sixteen he got his driver's license. Bob managed to buy an old Ford at a junkyard and had it towed to the alley behind our house. He discovered that the engine was no good, so he went back to the junkyard and bought another one of the same kind of car. This time the engine was good but the body was shot. He also had this car towed to the alley behind our house. Eventually, with a couple of older friends, he lifted the bad engine out with the help of a crane and a pulley. He managed to put the good engine in the car with the good body and had the old car towed away. Now he had one decent car with a good engine and a good body.

Agnes learning to drive

We were able to take our parents for a ride in the car every Sunday to the western suburbs. Father would always have a map, as he was the navigator. He would sit in the front seat next to the driver, and Mother and the kids would sit in the back seat. We usually stopped for ice cream or hot dogs after a Sunday afternoon cruise. It was very entertaining. I wasn't old enough to drive.

I learned to drive myself in the army during the war years. When I came back from the service, I managed to buy a cheap car, a 1937 Plymouth. I used it for a number of years. I would drive my parents around to a wake, or a meeting somewhere, and take Mother shopping.

Mother got enthralled by the idea that if she could drive a car, she could be independent. So she asked me if I would teach her how to drive. I agreed with some trepidation because I knew she had no idea about a car, what makes it go and stop, but I was willing to give her a try. Sure, Mom!

We drove out to the town of Westchester. In those days the town had been all laid out and a lot of houses were there. However, the Depression came along, and they never finished all the other houses so there was block after block of empty streets. No houses so you could see every which way at an intersection. It was an ideal place to teach someone to drive a car because hardly anybody was there except maybe somebody else learning to drive.

I first parked the car along a long stretch of a street, and I gave her a little sermon about how the brakes and the clutch worked. In those days you had a brake and a clutch and a gas pedal and a gear shift lever you had to shift.

I showed her how to shift to second gear and third gear and neutral. It was a complicated thing, and it mystified Mother but she still wanted to try it. So I said,

"You gotta stay on your side of the street in case other traffic is coming. The right side of the street at all times." She started off and instead of looking out the windshield, she kept looking at her feet because she wanted to see how the pedals were working. The clutch pedal was different from the brake pedal, so she was never looking out the window——she kept looking at her shoes. I said,

"Mom, you gotta look out the window so you don't bump into another car or people!" She said, "Yeah, okay," and I showed her how to stop the car and again she would be driving the car and looking at her feet instead of looking out the window. Just then a police car happened by this time. She was in the middle of the road as usual. I couldn't keep her by the right side of the road because she was hardly steering, just looking at her feet.

This was her first lesson mind you. Mother was deathly afraid of policemen for some reason. It must have been some childhood experience. She thought the law was a menacing presence. She didn't want to be arrested. So she's driving along in the middle of the street, and here come the cops pulling up from the other direction on the other side. They were hugging the street on the other side. The cops tooted their horn to get us to stop, and we did stop. The officer leaned out the window and said in a very friendly voice,

"Hey lady, you are going to have to drive on your side of the street, okay?" And my mother said, "Yes sir." She was very embarrassed by the whole thing and afraid of being arrested. The cop went on his merry way when he realized what was going on. Here was this middle-aged lady trying to learn how to drive a car and her son was trying to teach her. She said,

"Well, I've had it." I helped her pull over. She said, "I don't want to drive a car; it's not for me. Let's go home."

She was always in awe that I could drive car. I was twenty years old, and she saw me driving expertly and parking perfectly at the curb. She thought in her mind, "Well I could do that!" and of course it turned out to be a disaster.

Mother never again wanted to drive a car. I invited her a few more times. I told her it will be better each time; you'll learn a little bit more. She said,

"No, no, no. I don't need to drive a car. I can always get a ride from someone." That was my mother's big adventure. She probably drove half a mile at most. Her first and only driving experience. And I admire her pluck for trying.

I was born in 1925 at Oak Park Hospital a few blocks away from where our family lived in Forest Park, just west of Harlem Avenue and just south of the Eisenhower Expressway, which wasn't there in those days.

As a preschool kid, I was a little small for my age but I was smart and that helped me get along with bigger and tougher kids. I have happy memories of my preschool days and my devoted mother and father. I've got to say that my youth was a happy one.

In my youth, I fell in love with the game of softball and I remember playing when I was six. I remember, my older brother, Bob, who was three years older than me, showed me how to swing the bat in our backyard, and he would lob the ball to me. Every day after school or in the summer time we would play. I was a natural left-hander but I learned how to bat right-handed, out of necessity. Right field was always foul because we didn't have enough players to fill a whole field. I learned how to bat right-handed, but I still threw the ball left-handed, so it was very confusing to other people.

Funny thing. In those days, being left-handed was considered a problem. The desks were set up in such a way that the ink wells that we used were on the right side. My mother made a deal with the nun teaching first grade that my mother would bandage my left hand, all my fingers, and threaten me with severe consequences if I took the bandage off. I knew what it was about. I had to learn how to write with my right hand, not my left hand. I was trying hard to write with my left hand, and I couldn't do it because of the bandage. Eventually I learned how to write awkwardly with my left hand, and I gave up all together and learned to write with my right hand.

I had a number of friends and one of them was called Don. We got along great, but one time we were mad at each over some minor something—-I don't even remember what it was—-and my older brother Bob decided that he would arrange a grudge boxing match between me and my friend Don. Don was a bigger, stronger kid. I wasn't too keen about my chances at boxing Don, but Don was willing to go along. Neither one of us really wanted to fight, and we didn't know anything about boxing, but somehow we got some boxing gloves and a bunch of kids gathered around in this field where Don and I were going to square off.

We started reluctantly because we still liked each other really, but Bob was egging us on. It started with Don swinging a round house right at me, and in his awkwardness, he missed my face but his right elbow came around and hit me square in the nose. My nose started bleeding profusely down the front of my shirt and my chin and of course that ended the match then and there.

The fans were disappointed at the less-than-interesting fight, but I was bleeding too much to continue it. My brother Bob was disappointed because he was telling everybody I was going to beat up Don. But Don and I resumed our friendship as if nothing had happened.

I've talked about my youth and all, and it was an ordinary, happy time at school. I went to grammar school at St. Bernadine Church, a half a block away from where I lived on Elgin Avenue, very convenient. Starting in the fourth grade, I became an altar boy, that was the standard there. I was an altar boy then all through grade school and high school.

As an altar boy I was scheduled to be the server with one or two other kids at the six-thirty A.M. mass on a weekday. There was a church bell rung at six-thirty by pulling on a long rope, and the altar boy would ring it so people would know it was time to get to Mass.

Our parish added a new priest named Father Kenneth. He was just out of the seminary, maybe twenty-eight years old and very pious. A very nice young man but it seemed to us servers that he had a hard time waking up in the morning to be on time for the Mass. It was our job to ring the bell, and he would always come running in late, looking like he hadn't shaved, running up to the back steps getting dressed for the Mass. He would be maybe sound asleep, and he would hear the church bell ringing, and we could just imagine him jumping out of bed and throwing his clothes on to get there at maybe six-thirty-one. It amused me a great deal. He coached our basketball team in grammar school, and I admired him greatly. A good guy who liked to help all the parishioners. I was really in awe of him.

In the wintertime when the air was dry, it gave off static during the Mass. There would be a lot of static electricity generated by his shoes going down the carpeting in this very dry air, and we discovered, to our amusement, that when he got to the Communion rail to give out the Communion wafers, the first time he touched someone's tongue, there would be static shock. He shuffled his feet real fast on the carpeting.

Of course we didn't laugh or anything; we'd keep our mouths shut. We watched day after day when this would be going on, and people began to get wise to the fact that the first one in line was going to get a static shock. We could see that, in the cluster of people, the regulars were avoiding the first position. They didn't want to be the one to get shocked. Politely letting some little old lady or some visitor get up there first. Not very Christian.

I don't know if Father Kenneth was aware of it or not. We never mentioned it. It was funny to hear the snap of it and to watch their expressions.

I really was impressed with him, so when it was time for confirmation in seventh grade, I took the name Kenneth as my confirmation name in honor of him. And that's when one thing led to another and that's when I started thinking of being a priest like him. I told my parents I wanted to go to Quigley Preparatory Seminary after I graduated from grammar school.

They were very proud and pleased that one of their boys was going to be a priest one day. Which never happened, as you do know. But I did stay at Quigley for three years and got a great education and learned how to write. Had a lot of fun and friends. And Father Kenneth was my inspiration.

My parents were very excited about my decision, and my pastor also had to agree that I was suited to go to Quigley Preparatory Seminary. I had a long commute every day on the train, which in those days was called the Elevated and today called the CTA, from Forest Park all the way down to Clark and Lake Street, getting off there and walking about a mile and a half north to Quigley with a bunch of amazing nice young boys, of all whom thought they possibly wanted to be priests someday. It was a very scary experience for a thirteen-year-old kid, starting in such an auspicious building and a beautiful chapel with French architecture.

As I remember, there were forty in each class and seven classes. You were placed in your class alphabetically. It cost two cents for a bowl of soup at the cafeteria. We were expected to go to Mass every morning, either at Quigley or our home parish. I used to typically go to the six-thirty Mass in Forest Park and had to get up early before Father, though Mother may have been up then. I'd go off to Mass in the dark, and there was hardly anybody there, but they always had it and they rang the church bell.

At Quigley it was all priests teaching the children. There were no women, no lay people except a janitor or two. We had all the usual courses and then some. We had the usual amount of math, a moderate amount of science, and a lot of it was English language and different languages. I remember that in my first year, in addition to English, I had Latin. Starting in the second year, they added Greek. Also in the second year, I studied Bohemian [the language of the Czech Republic] once a week with a visiting Bohemian-speaking priest.

You were put in that class by your ethnicity. The kids who were Irish or whatever were typically put into a French class. I discovered quickly that there were fifteen or twenty boys in my Bohemian language class, and I was the only one who never spoke Bohemian at home with my parents.

One of the assignments in Bohemian class was to memorize the "Our Father" in Bohemian. Probably all rest of the boys in the class already knew the "Our Father" in Bohemian but I did not know it, and I had the text there and it was like Chinese to me. There were certain sounds I couldn't pronounce.

I remember one night I was in my room trying to memorize the "Our Father," and I could barely pronounce it, let alone memorize it by heart. I was having a hard time studying it, and Mother happened by and heard me talking in there. She knocked on the door and came in and said,

"What are you doing George?" and I said,

"Well I'm trying to memorize the 'Our Father' in Bohemian." She said, "That's nice." My mother knew that I didn't know Bohemian. She said,

"Maybe I can help you." I said,

"No, no, no, you'd just laugh!" and she said,

"Oh no, I would never laugh. I know it would be hard for you to learn the Bohemian language." My parents knew it and spoke to each other when we were younger kids, and they could speak freely in Bohemian about something going on when they didn't want the kids to understand. So I knew that I heard her speak Bohemian sometimes with other adults. So she said,

"Oh no, George, I would never laugh," and she said, "Why don't you start saying it and then maybe I can help you along a little bit." I said,

"No, no, no, just leave me alone. I have to memorize it myself," and she said,

"You start saying it, and I would never laugh because I know it's hard for you." So I started to say the "Our Father" in Bohemian, and I only got about four or five words out, and she burst out laughing because it sounded so bad. She couldn't stop herself.

My accent had very little bearing on how a Bohemian native speaker would say those words. But the priest who led the class didn't pick on me or laugh at me. He gave me a lot of leeway. He knew I didn't know much. He would call on me occasionally. He was a nice gentlemen.

So one year I'm studying English, not only English literature but how to write, and I was also learning Latin and Greek and Bohemian, all at the same time. The first couple of years I was very enthused about becoming a priest one day and I studied very hard. We had Thursdays off, and we went to school on Saturdays. It was very odd that they didn't want us running with the herd on the weekends. Girls! There might be girls around. They wanted us to have no girlfriends. They wanted us one day to be celibate priests. That was their hope and the whole point of this thing, so every Thursday I'd be home alone except I could look up a friend or two from Quigley. Only one lived reasonably near my home in Oak Park. Thursdays were kind of boring days. I spent the day catching up on my homework.

Besides going to school on Saturday, I was picked to be in the boy's choir in my freshman year. It was really based on whether your voice had changed or not. My voice had really not changed, so I was a typical boy soprano in those days.

But toward the end of my years at Quigley, I started to believe that I didn't have a vocation to be a priest anymore, and I found I was losing interest in my studies in my third year. It was a very tough year. People were expected to study three hours every night. I thought I was going to be a priest, but I figured out it was not for me. I became less and less enthused about the idea and I had to break the news to my parents.

I still go to reunions of the Quigley Alumni club. Most of the friends I had who became priests are dead already and the ones who didn't become priests, most of them are gone, and I'm still buzzing along somehow.

BASIC TRAINING
AND HEADING
TO EUROPE

Like all healthy young men during World War II, I was drafted. I was enlisted in the Navy for half an hour.

In my senior year at St. Patrick High School, two senior officers, one from the Army and one from the Navy, gave a test to the men in our class. They were looking for good students to enroll in a program called the "Specialized Training Program for College Studies" to be future officers and engineers and linguists. The idea was to preserve everybody of college quality from being drafted or forced to carry a rifle.

The Army had its own reasons to keep up a steady flow of officers, thinking that the war could go on for three or four more years for all they knew. They didn't want to empty the colleges of all the smart people and have no further source of the quality of people they were talking about.

When taking this test, you were asked to indicate your preference for either Army or Navy, and since my father had been in the Army in World War I and told a lot of stories over the dinner table about what it was like, I came to dislike the idea of the Navy and especially all that water. It seemed foreign to me. So I indicated Army for specialized training. Lo and behold, five of us from my senior class passed this test for the Army side, and I got a nice letter from the Army saying that I would do my country a favor and advance my military career if I were to join the Army Reserves and not active Army service.

The program was that you would be sent to college for a period of time, and depending on your skills, you would take a different kind of courses. The idea, for public relations purposes, was they first wanted to make a soldier out of you if you were in the Army or a sailor in the Navy because the public at large would say, "What are these guys doing in college? Why aren't they in the Army?"

I was still seventeen. The Army offered to send me immediately to college in civilian clothes and when I turned eighteen, I would be alerted to active duty. At that point the Army would give me basic training to make me a soldier and, if I succeeded, I would be sent back to college indefinitely in uniform.

I thought to myself, "Gee, that's wonderful," but I didn't have the money for the appropriate clothing for college. I didn't want to ask my parents for the money for clothes, so I decided not to fret about it, and I decided not to join but to wait until the Army drafted me.

The Army sent me a postcard that said that George Zak had passed the Army Specialized Training Program qualifications and that should be considered if he was drafted. So I kept that card, and it was like June when I got this letter. In September, I would be turning eighteen, and I figured I would only be in college for one quarter and it would not be worth the hassle.

So I declined, I just kept that card, and sure enough after I turned eighteen, I registered at the local post office as a future soldier or sailor to be drafted, and by November I was drafted. When I got to the classification department in downtown Chicago to pass the physical and so forth, they said,

"Well, you're in the Navy now." I said,

"Hunh? But I selected Army." And they said,

"Well, why would you want to be in the Army instead of the Navy? Sailor, sit over there and we'll make you an Army man."

Several officers and an enlisted man came over and interviewed me, and they wanted to know why in the world would I want to be in the Army instead of the Navy. I said,

"Well, my father was in the Army in World War I." I didn't mention that I passed the Army Specialized Training Program and figured that they weren't interested in that. I figured that they wanted to put me into the Navy for whatever reason they had. The Navy had so many slots to fill and I was a good one to fill it.

They finally gave up on it and they said,

"Alright. If that's the way you feel." They took out a big rubber stamp and they scratched out where it had been stamped "Navy" on the first page and they blotted all that out, and they took out another that said "Army."

"Sailor, you're in the Army now. Now get in line over there." That's how I was in the Navy for half an hour. From time to time, I wonder what life would have been like in the Navy.

For one thing, they didn't shut down the Navy college program. In the Navy, I probably would have gone to college for six months

George in uniform in Army basic training

to a year, more, or I might have been assigned to a ship and been torpedoed. I might have drowned in the ocean somewhere.

I had an exemplary career in the Navy. No problems. No demerits. Yes, for the half an hour that I was in the Navy.

In the Army, I was assigned to a combat infantry basic training program in Georgia. I was a skinny underweight guy but otherwise healthy. In due course, you learn how to safely fire a rifle and how to take it apart and do it safely. We camped in tents doing nothing but getting better and better at firing with better accuracy with rifles. Eventually, all 160 guys in our class passed. They were now accurate rifleman. They knew how to load it. Fire it. All the accurate safety precautions.

In combat our job was to be as close to the machine gun without being too close. Our job was to stay close or we would be a big target for the enemy. A big cluster of guys. We would spread out. We would be in ten running steps of the machine gun. So we couldn't carry a big heavy rifle; it would just be in our way.

Our way was to carry a carbine with a sling so it would be on our shoulder out of the way. Ready to be used. Fully loaded when necessary. So it got to be that I really fell in love with that carbine.

One time I was getting real good at it. I was assigned to a carbine range for the day to catch up on the practice. I walked to the place and we were assigned three guys to a target. The target was like three football fields away—-three hundred yards away.

The targets were manipulated by guys in an open trench. It was a big frame. Ten feet by ten feet with a big bull's-eye on it, and there would be like fifty of those in a row in a field. All along the trench there were guys whose job it was to be in the pits. When the bullet would hit the paper target that was the signal, and you would only shoot one at a time. That was the signal to the guy operating the little device there to lower the target, and he would take a little marker about four inches in diameter and put that on the target and roll the cable and make the target go up again so you could see where the bullet went in. Was it a bull's-eye or did it go somewhere else? It was a very slow process.

You had two guys and you'd take turns. Then the target would be lowered and the target would go up again. That went on for hours and it was very boring. We were pretty good shots and we had no problem hitting the bull's-eye from three hundred yards away. Lying prone. With the carbine.

So we thought of a way to make it more interesting. We decided to shoot the target to the left of us. So the guys would be ready to shoot and the target would go down. And the guys would be following the target down with their rifles as it was descending.

I dearly loved that carbine. I was proud of the fact that I had twelve out of fifteen bull's-eyes on the English shooting range. It was quite a long distance. You had fifteen shots and I got twelve out of fifteen.

After I finished the sergeant came out holding my sheet and said,

"Who is that guy? He got twelve out of fifteen." I proudly had to answer it was me. My sergeant came over. I thought he was going to congratulate me. All he wanted to do was take down the serial number of my carbine in case they needed a carbine that was reliable.

No, he didn't say anything. He said, "Give me that." He could have said, "Nice going, George." He just took down the number.

After about three and a half months of vigorous training, lots of running, jumping, carrying heavy loads, and learning how to fire weapons, I grew both in height and weight and put on about thirty pounds of muscle. I got up to about 155 pounds.

I learned a number of ways to kill other people and avoid being killed. And that's what basic training was all about. I learned how to throw hand grenades, how to fire a bazooka, a tank gun. I learned how to fire a carbine accurately, which is a short rifle, and the M1, which is the longer one. Learned how to use a bayonet and charge after somebody and move against them and try to knock the other guy's rifle aside and then jab my own bayonet into him.

Of course, it was not my nature to do this. I was not an angry or hateful man. I was young, still a boy of eighteen, but it was my duty to serve my country. Of course I could have stayed in the seminary system and waited out the war that way. But I wouldn't have done that. I wanted to be honest to myself and to my country.

By the time I finished my basic training, I was very fit and strong, but I realized that I was in the infantry for good and that most of the casualties are in the infantry. There are other ways of getting killed in the services, but the infantry took the brunt of the casualties. This was not the way that I thought my life was going to go, but there I was and I'd do my best and do my duty.

I was finally transferred after basic training to Indiana, to a place called Camp Addenbery. As a part of the 106th Infantry Division, my basic training in Georgia was over, and now here I was in Camp Addenbery, joining a new division. It consisted of about fourteen thousand men including officers. We would have our own artillery attached to our division, but most of us were riflemen or machine gunners or mortar men or medics.

I was next sent back to Georgia, to Fort Benning. We were all placed in open slots in the division that had just finished maneuvers in Tennessee. They were up to speed as individual soldiers, well trained, and experienced. About seven thousand of them had been shipped to places such as Italy. Guys like me were sent in to replace these men, gone, possibly forever.

I remember hearing after the war that the captain of our basic training group was killed in Italy commanding soldiers there. It broke my heart, because he was a nice guy but firm and well suited to his job.

I got tougher and stronger through my basic infantry training, and I had a couple of furloughs home and I was very proud to show up in my uniform. I ended my furloughs all too soon. I had a wonderful time and I was ready to take on my duties.

After I returned to Fort Benning from my furlough, my company commander asked us for volunteers for the motor pool. In the army there is an old saying, "Never volunteer because you'll be sorry." I decided to go against that bit of common wisdom. He said anybody who wants to work in the motor pool for a temporary assignment of about a month step forward.

First of all, I was tired of all the hard work I was doing, and second, I was fascinated with vehicles. Jeeps were always coming and going and I thought, "Gee, I'd sure like to see what it feels like to drive one of those." The trouble was, I didn't know how to drive. Ha. I had driven my brother Bob's car a couple of times in a parking lot. Just in a circle around the parking lot in the summer time, and he told me now shift this way and shift that way. I'd had only five minutes of driving time, I think, and that was my entire experience driving a car.

I thought, "Well maybe if I can get in the motor pool, I can become a jeep driver and that would be a lot better than all this heavy back-breaking work I'm doing." I stepped forward and a whole bunch of other guys did too. They explained that the jeeps had been on maneuvers, so they'd been in the mud and were in real bad shape. They needed overhaul and a place to take them apart. These jeeps weren't going to be going anywhere and they had to be worked on.

There were nineteen jeeps assigned to our company, a heavy artillery company. And one three-quarter-ton Dodge truck, which was a small truck for a mechanic in which to keep all his tools and spare parts for nineteen jeeps and fourteen two-wheeled trailers.

The motor sergeant went from man to man to see who would be good for him. He was in charge of all the company's jeeps. He went to each guy in turn and asked him what he knew about jeeps, cars, and stuff. When he got to me, he asked me how much driving experience I had. I said,

"Sir, I drove every chance I got." I didn't tell him it was two five-minute spots. He said,

"Okay get over there." We were sent to the motor pool filled with row upon row of jeeps and, sure enough, these jeeps were in bad shape. Some of them had been damaged a little bit, but most of them were dirty and rusty looking. Yep, these jeeps weren't going anywhere. We were given the job of taking off anything that could come off. Jack 'em up. Take off the tires. Replace the tires. We learned how to put tires on a certain way. We learned how to take off anything that was removable except for the engine, the starter, and the generator.

That was the first time I learned anything about a motor vehicle. It turned out the jeep was a strong but simple vehicle. It didn't take me long to figure out what all this was about.

Two of us were assigned to each jeep, and every morning when everybody else was going to run through the woods, we marched over to the motor pool and spent the whole day there. Repainting and sanding and what-not.

When I got a chance I'd get into that vehicle and put it into first gear and make it go forward for about five feet, and then put it in reverse and go ten feet, just to get the feel of how to use the clutch and the gear shift.

Each gear shift has a different position. The gear shift level was on the floor, and there were also two other gear shifts. Smaller ones. One was to turn it into a four-wheel drive vehicle, and the other was to put it into a low-gear ratio, which meant that all the power was coming into the vehicle but it couldn't go too fast. This was good for crawling through the mud or up a hill because all the power was concentrated in the first or second gear.

I was starting to master all that stuff without letting anybody know I hadn't driven a car before. After a while, I got to the point where I could drive the car over to the grease rack and drive it up on the rack and get the grease gun and grease up the points under the jeep and so forth. I was having a great time driving it back and forth, and finally we were given a two-week training school.

Not everybody was invited to the school. There were two of us for each vehicle, and they picked out the one that seemed to be the most dedicated and smart and all that, and I was one of them picked. The two-week school was right there, to learn the finer points of driving a jeep and a trailer that went with it. I ended up being a licensed jeep driver.

In school, we had lectures and demonstrations about the care and maintenance of jeeps and how to shift to low gear. I had a few turns on a three-quarter-ton truck and also the massive two-and-a-half-ton truck, which were commonly used for transporting troops or shipping materials.

One day during training I was driving along in this convoy, the last one in a stream of about twenty jeeps. Two passengers were with me, and we were going on a road I had driven before. In a convoy, it's more like an accordion, because if the drivers fail to keep the proper distance between vehicles, they slow down, they bunch up, then spread out as they are driven.

We were on a steep hill, and at the bottom I was supposed to take a hard left to go over a bridge. My lieutenant's jeep was parked at the bottom of the hill, to ensure that we all turned left onto the bridge. To my horror, I can see his jeep is parked sideways, blocking the road so you can't go straight ahead, and I'm picking up speed, going faster and faster, and I'm pumping the brake like mad but can't get the jeep to slow down. The lieutenant's just standing on the bridge with his hands on his hips, watching the other jeeps go by, all of them turning left onto the bridge, but my jeep wasn't slowing down. I was clearly going to hit the lieutenant's jeep for sure, and my passenger and I would be killed.

I kept leaning on the brake as hard as I could—really standing on the brake. I just whipped the wheel to the left just as we got short of the lieutenant's jeep, and at the last second, our jeep skidded sideways just about colliding, but we made it and went zooming over the bridge. I managed to survive all that and I was thanking my lucky stars that nothing bad had happened.

That was a real heart stopper. I'd told my sergeant that my jeep's brake pads were bad, but he'd just told me to make do.

I remember another time that I almost had a bad collision driving a lieutenant to some meeting, and I was traveling on an unfamiliar road. I could see there was a hill, and at the bottom of the hill, it turned right to go around the hill. An "S" turn. First I had to turn right, and then about two hundred feet down was another turn around to the left. So I was zooming along pretty fast when I realized what was coming was a sharp "S" turn, so I make my right turn, and all of a sudden around the bend coming at me is a two-and-a-half-ton truck taking up all the road, and we are headed for a head-on collision.

So the driver of the truck smartly got over to his side and hugged the side of the hill as close as he could. And I was coming along, and to the right of me was a ditch, and if I was to drive down the road into the ditch, the jeep would have turned upside down in the ditch and the lieutenant and I would have both been killed. So I'm driving along with my head out the side, no top just the windshield, and I'm driving with my head and my ears closest to the tires of the truck I could get without touching them, and we zoomed by each other with a couple of inches to spare at the most.

Then I quickly had to make a left turn. Luckily there was no more traffic coming, and the truck went on its way and I went on my way. I could hardly catch my breath. But I was very proud of both of us. I didn't go into the ditch. I didn't crash into him, and I got the closest to his tires as I actually could without touching them.

We passed in a flash like that. We could hardly breathe, and now I'm slowing down, and the lieutenant got his heart pumping down, and he says,

"Do you always drive like that?" I saved both our lives by skillful driving, by driving this jeep as close as possible without hitting the truck and not going in the ditch, and of course there wasn't a scratch on the truck or the jeep, and he didn't go any further. He could have reported me for being a dangerous driver but he didn't.

I learned my lesson. You don't assume anything when you are driving any kind of a car. A lesson I kept and took into my civilian life later. You never do anything by just guess work. I should have slowed down when I was coming to this strange hill up ahead, but I didn't until I turned the corner and saw the truck coming at me in the other direction.

My division was fourteen thousand strong, and we were pointed to points unknown. We thought we were going to be taken by train. We didn't know for sure, but that's how it turned out. We finally got our orders to go by train, and we went by train to Camp Miles Standish near Boston. After a few days we went by train to New York, and then we went directly by small boats to the New Jersey side of the river where the docks were, and I recall getting into the small boats with a whole bunch of other guys. It was not a normal kind of boat, it was clearly a boat where the bottom could open up.

It might have been like a garbage scow. I could imagine it being filled with trash and that being towed out to the ocean or whatever, and out it would spill all this stuff. I could see all these gears squashed in the bottom of this thing. If somebody made the wrong move, you could get squashed in the bottom of this thing. We could all be dumped into the bottom of the water. That didn't happen, but it was a makeshift way of getting us across the river. They had all fourteen thousand of us to transfer, and I am sure that others went by other kinds of boat or whatever.

We transferred to this open boat at the dock. It turned out that it was an English ship about thirty years old at the time. In its heyday, it had been the ship of choice for rich people crossing the Atlantic Ocean between World War I and World War II. It had been a luxury ship, but now it had been converted into a ship to transfer troops, and it made trips all over the world.

We were all us were shocked at the size of the ship. It was gigantic. After a certain amount of confusion and all, we were lined up onto the ship. And I remember there were seven decks on the ship. All the way down to "G" deck. I never got down that far. I was lucky. Our company of 165 men was in "B" deck. That was the best deck to be in, above the water line. All of the rest of the decks were below the water line.

Our deck "B" was shorter across the back, and we were put into what had been a ballroom of some kind in its day. It must have been the center of activity for all the wealthy people crossing the Atlantic, and now there were five high bunks squashed in. I think I was in the fourth or fifth from the bottom, but the nice part about it was that we could walk out the door on "B" deck and have fresh air right there on the deck surrounding the quarters itself.

Below that was the "C" deck, which stretched to the rear of the ship. Because they didn't want any unusual weight one way or the other, there was a line across the middle of the ship, and we were not allowed to cross. Eventually we arrived in England.

England is a very interesting place. I remember seeing the countryside on the way in from the harbor. Our staff sergeants led us in slightly bawdy songs to pass the time, and we were all in good spirits and all the while wondering what was going to be happening.

Our camp was called Stow-on-the-Wold in an area of England called the Cotswolds. Our camp consisted of a bunch of metal huts, each with a coal-burning stove. It was November, it was cold and damp and getting colder it seemed by the day. We did light training and all that to pass the time. I weighed myself somehow. I weighed 155 pounds, I remember, and felt strong and fit.

One day we went to the carbine range to get a little more practice with our carbines. We each had one clip of fifteen bullets to shoot, one after the other at this one target, three hundred yards away. I had my few minutes of fame when I got twelve bull's-eyes, and I was very pleased with that. My good old carbine was in good hands I thought.

Within this three-month's time, I got a three-day pass. I guess everybody did, in groups. I made a buddy and we made a quick bus trip to various cities. We went to Stratford-upon-Avon, where we stayed overnight, and we also went to Coventry and Warwick Castle.

We found a play at the Stratford-upon-Avon theater. There was hardly anybody in the theater except GIs like myself. Everybody was on duty somewhere in the military. We got to the city of Coventry, which was famous for being bombed by the Germans in 1940 at the beginning of the war when Germany just plastered this famous cathedral.

My buddy Jack and I got there somehow, and we walked among the rubble just the way it was. The bombers had never come back. There was some roof and some walls, but it was just as it was. The floor itself was about five feet high with junk. Boulders, big stone pieces from the ceiling, and big beams that had been the ceiling. it was very sad to think that this terrible destruction took place.

I want to mention that after the war, many years after the war, after I retired, Mother and I took a trip to see all the countries in the British Isles. We visited the ruins of Coventry Cathedral. They had gotten rid of the five-foot pile of debris from the collapsed roof of the building and all the loose parts of the wall and that glass on the floor of the cathedral. There was like a park bench where you could sit and contemplate adjacent to the ruined church. After the war, a brand-new Coventry Cathedral was built, but they left the old wreckage where it was. The new cathedral is modern and beautiful, and I thought that it was nice that I got to see it again.

About two weeks after my trip with Jack, we were issued live ammunition for our carbines. We had machine guns, and we were ready to be committed to the battle. So we were ready to begin our trip, but we didn't know where to.

THE BATTLE OF
THE BULGE

We were sent to a Landing Ship Tank, very famous in World War II. They had thousands of them manufactured, many in New Orleans. We sat on board the ship for three days in the English Channel, because there was heavy weather and we couldn't get out of the channel. We were going to go into the city of Le Havre, and then go up the Seine River.

The ship that I was on was filled with nothing but jeeps and trucks plus the drivers and assistant drivers like myself. The rest of the troops went on bigger ships across the channel. We finally got together on the coast of France up the river, and all around us we could see the devastation from the D-day fighting about five months before.

There were ships half sunk in the Seine and burned-out tanks and other tanks all over the landscape as we floated slowly down this river making our way to Rouen. That may ring a bell in your mind. That was the place where Joan of Arc was burned at the stake hundreds of years before.

When we got there, a ramp came down and we drove our jeep down and followed the convoy to a big farmer's field some miles away. We camped for a week or more while waiting for orders to move to Belgium. We finally did that and then we left and I was a back-seat passenger in a jeep for about a week. The regular driver for our squad drove all the way across France, and our squad corporal sat in the passenger seat.

Every once in a while along the way, there would be a big red ball painted on the side of a tree or a fence, telling you were on the right route. They called the route the "red ball express." It was a one-way road, and it headed for the front line. If you were coming from the front line, there was another red ball express running parallel some miles away. It picked out the best way of getting to Belgium and to Germany.

We arrived at just a place in the woods in Belgium, and it was bitter, bitter cold, December, and I wished I had more clothes. I wished I had something like a mask for my face. There was none to be had. We all suffered from the cold. We couldn't have the top up or the windshield up on the jeep because the windshield was on a hinge forward and that was latched down. We slept the night the three of us in the jeep, and we woke up in the morning covered in snow in the bitter cold. It was pretty miserable. It was really tough.

We finally arrived in a now-famous town called St. Vith. Every veteran of the Battle of the Bulge knows St. Vith. We drove into this very quaint, interesting town in the convoy, and I couldn't see a scratch on that whole town. There was no sign of any fighting in the town.

But as we drove through the town very slowly, we were told to load our guns as we never knew what would happen—-we could be ambushed or something. Nobody knew that much about anything. Off the front to the east and to the southeast, we could see muzzle blasts of artillery fire going on and a booming and a bang of exploding shells, and we knew we were getting serious and we'd be getting into the combat zone before we knew it.

St. Vith's was the general headquarters in charge of our division. We made our way slowly through the town. Little did I know that later that town would be almost totally demolished in fighting between the Germans and the Americans in the Battle of the Bulge, but we were way further east of that at the time. St. Vith's held out for five or six days before what was left of the troops retreated out of there west before the Germans kept overwhelming everything.

We got to the east end of town and held up. There was an MP holding us up. We could hear an artillery shell exploding, and we came up to the crossroad and there lying in the ditch was the very first dead American I ever saw. Lying in a ditch. He had been killed by an artillery shell.

They had carried him over there obviously because he was spread-eagle face down. It was clear to me that the poor guy. . . . They had an arm or a leg and carried him over there, his body over to the side of the road face down. That was really getting grim. The only other dead soldier I saw before that was a guy killed in training back at Camp Addenbery in Indiana while going through an infiltration course firing over our heads. This poor guy apparently stood up and got a bullet between the eyes and was killed instantly.

We then gunned the motor and zoomed off, and we found ourselves making a right turn with a big sort of a mountain on our right side, which was called the Schnee Eifel. We finally got to a little road at the top of the hill, and we made our way to the top of the Schnee Eifel ridge, which was hundreds of feet above the rest of the hills in the area.

We were wondering whether we would get shot by artillery on the way there but we didn't. We got to the top and found our company, and the corporal and I got off the jeep and the jeep driver took off to where he came from and I never saw him again or the jeep. The jeep got blown up later with nobody in it. I found out that it was destroyed by a tank shell.

The Schnee Eifel ridge was a long ridge that extended north and south, and our squad was in charge of a machine gun nest on the top of the mountain looking down into a valley. At the bottom of the valley were four-foot-high concrete posts, hundreds of them lined up to prevent trucks from getting through there. The Germans were camped on that side across this big open valley with the concrete barriers separating the two armies, and we were on the other side.

There was no fighting going on, but they would occasionally shoot an artillery shell or two whizzing over our heads into the German side——whatever target they were shooting at, I had no idea. We could hear the firing and hear the mumbled flashes and it was kind of scary.

But here's the odd thing. We had inherited this whole front from another division, the Second Infantry Division, and they had inherited it several months earlier from the Fourth Infantry Division. The Fourth Infantry Division actually captured this whole area from the Germans and then they moved out somewhere else and their spot was taken over by the Second Division. And they'd been there for a couple of months and nothing much was happening.

It was all filled with Christmas-like trees, everywhere you looked. Trees. Trees. Trees. No place for a road. The company had set up an outdoor cooking spot for the cooks. We took turns on patrolling duty. The guys from Second Infantry who were still there waiting to be picked up told us we would have it easy here because they had had it easy there for two months. Nothing much going on besides patrolling because the terrain was so rough. British and American high commands thought that there was no likelihood of an attack through where we were.

In the meantime, the British and Americans were preparing for an attack some miles to the south of us and some miles to the north of us. We were on this ridge spread out over about fifteen miles from north to south. It bothered me when it was my turn to be in the machine gun nest with a buddy looking down the valley watching for Germans. My buddy and I were the entire American front line at that point. There was nobody behind us except down in the valley way beyond the ridge, and we were more like a long daisy chain of watchmen. When I was in that machine gun nest, I couldn't hear or see any American to my left or to my right. That's how far apart we were spaced, and as I said, we were really there as lookouts.

They didn't want to have a division only four or five miles in the front of defense, which was more typical. We had fifteen miles to watch over and that's why we were spread out so thin. A part of our division was our artillery way behind us near St. Vith's, but we were actually in Germany and our headquarters at St. Vith's was four or five miles behind us back inside of Belgium.

The deal was we were on duty for two hours in the machine gun nest and then we'd be off for four hours. In that four hours we could either go into an underground bunker that the previous guys had built there or go get a meal or whatever. That was twenty-four hours a day, two on and four off.

We got there, say, on the ninth of December and the Germans finally attacked on the sixteenth. We were getting used to the place, and except for artillery firing over our heads, nobody was firing right at us except this one time. We could hear machine gun fire going on, the rat-a-tat-tat stuff going on. Day and night. It was probably patrols to see if the enemy was coming in the darkness.

There were evergreens all over and cold. Bitter, bitter, ice cold, and I just couldn't get warm at all and this underground hut that we had was just a big hole dug in the ground: ten or twelve feet wide and maybe eight feet deep, covered on top with heavy logs that the soldiers had sawed down from trees over time and hauled up there and placed over it and put sand bags on top of it in case it got hit by artillery. There was a good chance we wouldn't survive if it was hit and we were in the bunker. It was really worrisome.

We slept with our loaded carbines at our sides when we were off duty and nothing much was happening. Little did we know the Germans were secretly coming to the front. Not only in front of us but it turned out there was a road that had come to the south of us, which we had come across in our jeep, and come north up to where our actual company was and some miles south there was another road coming through this mountain. When we initially arrived at the front, we could hear the sound of trucks on that German side on the next ridge. We reported that to our sergeants, and I presume they told this to their officers who were back there somewhere, but nothing ever came of it.

It turned out the Germans were massing enormous forces, but their plan of attack, I found out later, was to leave us sitting up on the ridge. They drove their tanks and trucks and troops on foot to our north and to our south and joined behind the ridge including our artillery.

It all started at like five-thirty in the morning December 16, 1944. I'll never forget the date. I was in the bunker asleep. The Battle of the Bulge came on with a terrible roar. The Battle of the Bulge was quite the battle, but we didn't realize at the time that it was the beginning of an epic battle. We were just 425 members of our Company M, the Second Regiment of the 106th Division. We were new to battle and we hoped we knew what we were doing, and we hoped our officers knew what they were doing.

I was actually sleeping in the underground hut that the previous division had made. I was awakened inside my dirt hole by the roar of the German artillery exploding over our heads and exploding to our rear, and I assumed they were shooting at our artillery and storage division, which turned out to be true.

This was Hitler's idea by the way, this whole Battle of the Bulge idea, because nothing was going right, and Hitler felt that somehow to attack the American lines would force us out of the port of Antwerp where all our supplies were then coming in. If Hitler could then capture that port, we could no longer bring in food and ammunition and additional troops and artillery pieces from the port.

Hitler decided to take this gamble, which many of his generals felt was a hopeless idea. They had lost so many men and equipment running battles. For example, the Normandy battle on D day was five months before that. The Germans had lost a lot of everything. I'm telling you about things I read after the war but I didn't know at the time.

By Hitler's orders they had marshaled all the soldiers they could possibly find including Hitler Youth and old men and whatever wherever they were under the cover of a terrible foggy winter, which Hitler counted on. It was so foggy the American's side could not fly any observation planes and our bombers were socked in for the day. Luck was on Hitler's side in that respect when it started.

The whole thing hinged on Hitler punching through quick and surrounding guys like us where we were thinly spread and punch their way all the way to Antwerp before the American and British sides really knew was happening. The Allies really didn't think anything was going to happen. That would have given Hitler a big respite, and in his own demented mind, he could maybe imagine the Americans would join with him in fighting the Russians through Poland and whatnot.

It was all nonsense. The Americans came on very strong with all the troops and guns and artillery that the American side could ever dream of that they still had available.

At the beginning of this big battle, which I didn't even know was starting, it was overcast. Sooner or later our artillery started fighting back. Started whistling over our head. The Germans were firing behind us at our depots and artillery and we were firing our artillery behind the next ridge. It was chaos.

Then at that very first day we were stopped by buzz bombs, V-1 rockets. Imagine: twenty-five feet long and ten feet in diameter and a fin on top of it. It looked like a long, huge rocket. They had been landing in London intermittently. All of a sudden they were being launched behind the next ridge where the Germans had their launching ridge set up. The things were filled with explosives, and it was a very scary thing to watch flying overhead especially at night. Night and day they were going off one at a time. They were still gaining altitude as they were passing overhead, and they let a big flame out of the top of the launcher. The large part had a large wing on the side to help stabilize it.

The way it worked was, they aimed this thing on the launching pad and put in an amount of fuel they would estimate that it would take to go a certain distance in a certain exact direction from the launching pad toward, say, the Antwerp port, and this thing would go off and would simply fall to the earth when it ran out of gas. It would fall down and explode on whatever it landed on: soldiers, a house, or a port or ship. Very cruel. It was not a very accurate rocket, but it was very awesome and terrifying to watch this thing overhead. Later the V-2 rockets came along, and they were more devastating than this one. But not during the Battle of the Bulge.

The V-1s kept coming day and night and hitting targets in the rear. The GIs would call them "flying gas mains" because they looked like twenty-five-foot pipes with flames coming out of the back end. We watched them and worried and hoped that the engine wouldn't fall out and land on top of us. That went on for several days.

We were really worried about what was going to happen next. We didn't realize that we were actually cut off the very first day. The

Germans penetrated down the road to the north of us and to the south of us, and then joined behind us and cut us off completely. For several days we had no communication except for a little bit by radio with our headquarters back in St. Vith.

I had nothing to do with that. I was not involved. I was just a lowly private first class. Getting no food, no water, nothing. Our last meal I recall before the battle was a hot breakfast. I didn't eat for several days after that. All the water I had was in the canteen, plus all the snow I cared to eat because the ground was covered with snow. It was bitter, bitter cold.

I was taking my turn in the machine gun nest, not firing, just watching and waiting for German tanks and troops to come pouring down the ridge at the other side and then to give the alarm. But that never happened. One time I was crouched in the pit and a bullet swished right by my head, and it lodged in the log behind my head. I could feel a snap crack right behind my head. Just above my head. I couldn't figure out what they were aiming at. It was either someone with a telescopic scope deliberately aiming at the top of the ridge where they knew there were machine guns pointing down, or was it a stray shot. I have no idea. It went bam right in the log. That was the first day, the sixteenth.

The second day we were told by our higher command, the sergeant, that German paratroops had been reported landing in our rear. They were being routed and they were retreating back toward us on their way back over the hill to their positions. It was false information totally. There were German paratroopers who landed here and there, but nowhere near where we were.

We were told to get our machine guns and mortars out and point them backward in the opposite direction, back toward the top of the hill to aim at retreating German soldiers. Retreating from being overrun by us from the Americans behind us, down where the artillery was.

No paratroopers ever appeared. It was totally wrong, chaotic information. Then that night our squad had shifts around the clock watching for any Germans coming from our rear. It was just very bad.

We were now aware we were not getting any additional food or any water being brought up or anything else. We didn't know we were surrounded. It was more than just surrounded; we were just a small part of a much, much broader battle going to the south and the north of us. We were just two regiments totaling about maybe eight thousand men spread over fifteen miles and a lookout.

We were finally told that we were going to be pulling out at ten-thirty on the December the eighteenth. The battle started on the sixteenth and here it was two days later. We were told to get ourselves together and leave any personal items or letters from home in our duffel bags and take just what we could carry and nothing more, just our ammunition and hand grenades. We were going to try to break out of the encirclement.

We were all excited about this and what would happen next, so we were leaving very reluctantly our bags with extra clothes and extra socks and underwear and extra shirts and pants and extra pairs of shoes. I had a great big pair of duffel bags and put them all in trenches and left them there.

I remember one lieutenant told a sergeant to place a booby trap there with the bags. The sergeant refused. He said, "No. I won't do it." Because it was senseless killing of someone who was not attacking us directly after we had left. A booby trap near the bunch of bags is not fair in normal war. I felt the same way; I was ready to kill Germans, but not that way, by a cowardly booby trap.

We started lugging our stuff, and I felt like a pack mule. We all felt the same way. Not only did I have a full field pack, but I had boots, newly acquired over-boots. By that time my feet were already badly frozen but at least the boots kept more water and snow from coming in. I had an overcoat and the hard plastic liner on the steel helmet on my head, and a full field pack on my back, a rolled up raincoat and a sleeping bag but no pup tent; a gas mask on a large loop over my shoulder around my neck and on the other side I had other stuff I was carrying. On my back I had, besides the raincoat and the shelter pack, a small bag with some articles like a razor and an extra pair of socks, and on my other shoulder I was carrying on another belt my carbine and on another belt I had a wet belt in which I was carrying magazines for my carbines. A magazine is a metal box that you can slip in the bottom of a carbine to fire one bullet each time you press the trigger. In each hand I was carrying a heavy metal box carrying belts of ammunition for the machine gun.

That was my total job. Staying near the machine gun with the others in the squad doing the same thing. And one of the guys carried the machine gun and barrel, the other guy carried the bipod that went with it. Off we went like pack animals.

Even though it was bitter cold outside, because of all the stuff I was carrying, I started to sweat and feel the strain as we were making our way through the mud and snow and through the forest. I didn't know where we were heading. I hoped the ones who were leading us had some idea where we were going. But it turns out we were wandering not exactly in circles but not getting anywhere. It took all day to get about five miles from the beginning point to where we ended up. But we didn't see any German all that time.

I remember finally, we were all getting exhausted, and as I was going along I began to see discarded overcoats, hand grenades, all kinds of stuff thrown off because some guy couldn't carry it anymore. I finally threw off my gas mask and its carrying case. I threw away my hand grenades that I had in my overcoat. I was getting desperate. I was sweating and hot and still it was bitter cold whipping around my face.

Like everybody else I kept chucking stuff I couldn't carry anymore, but I held onto the precious stuff, the metal boxes. I finally stopped and took off the stuff around my neck and took off my overcoat and threw it away and put my carbine back over my shoulder.

And now I was wearing a lighter jacket, a fingertip jacket, there wasn't much lining to it, under my overcoat. I bitterly regretted later getting rid of my overcoat. But I just didn't know what to do to keep going.

By this time it was dark, and I tripped over a root on the ground and tripped down a little ravine and my helmet liner went flying in the dark, and I couldn't stop marching in the dark and look for it. That was the last of my steel helmet and hard plastic liner.

Later I tripped again and tumbled down a hill, and my sleeping bag came loose, and I had to cut it loose and get rid of it, and my raincoat was gone and I was really in a mess, but I still had my two ammunition boxes. That was my job to carry them wherever we were going.

Finally the word was given out that we were going to attack the Belgian town of Schönberg. We had started out in Germany. We had gone only a couple miles in Germany when we got to the front line.

Now we were back in Belgium, and in the morning we were going to attack Schönberg and recapture it from the Germans, and then somehow we were going to cross some kind of river and put up defensive positions. It sounded pretty impossible, but we were going to do what we were told to do.

To my amazement we didn't see any Germans at all along the way. Now it was pitch dark and we were told to stop and form a circle in the dark and start digging fox holes to sleep in for the night. I had a hatchet as my digging tool, and I started chopping through the snow and the ice and tree roots to make what we called a slit trench. It wasn't a deep hole; it was more like a shallow grave. It was like a foot and a half deep. After a time, a whisper came along the line, "We're moving out."

So all that work was for nothing. I picked up my boxes and off we went. We finally ended up in a field by a road, which looked like a farm field of some sort. We still saw no Germans, nobody, no traffic, nothing going on, but in the distance we could see flashes of artillery going off all night long. We posted guards by our group to watch out for any German troops coming.

I was one of those for the first hour's watch, and I was glad to be on the watch because I didn't have to lie down in the rain and snow without a raincoat to lie on. No sleeping bag, no nothing to lie on, nothing, just my rifle and my ammo belt and a few other things. My hour was up and all that time I'd been watching these V-1s go over in the dark. They were now somewhat higher up than when they were first launched. They were so eery, motor groaning—-rrrh, rhhh—-and this big flash of light came out the back, but it was clearly not heading for us. It was heading for somewhere in the rear area.

After my hour was up, I stood up for the rest of the night without any sleep whatsoever. Just stood around watching the V-1s going over head and hearing the booming of artillery off in the distance. I knew we were taking a shellacking from the Germans somewhere. I just didn't know what was going to happen next.

Morning came in the American Army. Our company finally resumed our march toward the town of Schönberg. We got to a high ridge looking down on the town. It was just after dawn when we got there. I thought, if we are going to attack this town, let's do it now while it's still semi-dark because the dark was still shielding us somewhat from the Germans who surely knew of our presence.

It turned out our commander, Commander Perkins, was waiting for orders which weren't coming. I remember seeing him on a little rise on the ground with a very grim, serious look on his face, surrounded by his officers. They were talking obviously about what was going to happen next, but they were waiting for orders to attack Schönberg along with other companies assembling nearby. And all that while I was thinking the Germans surely will see us from buildings. They were big farm buildings.

Not a German in sight, but in my mind I was imagining them wheeling up truckloads of ammunition for their artillery and what not and bringing more soldiers in and all the while we are sitting up there in full view and doing nothing except exposing us to the enemy looking out through windows and whatnot and from behind fences.

It was a really weird thing. The space between us and Schönberg was nothing but an open field looking gently downward to where the town actually started, and I was sure right behind those buildings and further back they had their artillery lined up and mortars lined up and their machine guns lined up ready to open up on us when we started our approach.

To pass the time I had a can of hot dogs cooked frozen, which I got off the LST ship. I remember opening my can with my dagger and passing out one hot dog to each guy in our squad. Each guy got one including myself. It was the first time I had had any food to eat since the day before.

Finally the order came, about ten o'clock in the morning, to advance onto Schönberg. We were going to come out of the woods, spread out and drive the Germans out of that town, take it over and set up our defense there to help us get out of the trap.

We were carrying all of our stuff, including our squad machine gun, and first we had to cross that big open farm field with no shelter of any kind. We had no artillery. No tanks. No air cover. Nothing. We just had our mortars and our machine guns. But there was no use setting it up because we didn't know where the enemy guns were to shoot at. We had to find out first by getting in the buildings. So totally surrounded and exhausted that it was bound to fail.

So down we marched, spread out, and headed down the slope to the field. As soon as we got out of the woods, we got rained on by falling artillery shells. They were ready for us.

Blam. Blam. Blam.

The guys were falling down screaming. Some of them obviously dead already. Machine gun bullets were whipping by and it was really hell. We could still see no Germans. They were firing the mortars over the building and onto us. There was nothing to shoot at. You'd be wasting your time shooting at the building.

We were just outgunned and outclassed. The tactics we were using, which we had nothing to do with, were totally hopeless and inadequate. The officers in charge I guess were doing their best under the worst possible conditions.

We were being bombarded by the artillery shells and the mortar shells and machine guns, and we were being slaughtered. And all this while machine gun bullets were whistling by my ear. None of them hit me but I could feel them whipping by, and it was like being in a shooting gallery waiting to be shot, you know. With men lying dead and dying all around me, I was one of the only beings still alive. It was a total disaster. We were totally outgunned, outsmarted every which way. Finally the order came to stop the advance and leave the dead and dying where they were and get back toward the woods we came from.

Those of us who weren't hurt finally made our way up the hill half a block and into the woods. Halfway into the woods, we were mortared again. All this time I didn't have a shot fired out of my carbine because there was no purpose to it at this point. I had to have a purpose to shoot it at some live soldier.

When we got into the woods, we finally came upon a clearing, and there we were all told to lie down to avoid any fire there of artillery or mortar shells. On the way there, my company commander,

Captain James Perkins, and my squad sergeant were standing up in the open woods in a clearing trying to decide which way to point our machine gun if the Germans came at us quickly. While they were doing that, the rest of us, the rest of our squad were flat on our bellies, trying to keep as low a profile as possible. All of a sudden mortar shells started exploding among all of us. The Germans were attacking us with mortars and also they were setting up their artillery but it wasn't ready yet.

The Germans were getting at us and these shells were exploding, and every time one would explode near me, lying on my stomach, I was bounced off the ground about a foot from the concussion and the power of the explosion into the ground as well. Of course I had no helmet and that wouldn't have done me much good. This went on for some time, and we were really getting a beating with these mortars or artillery shells. Bits of steel were buzzing all over the place whizzing over my head but they didn't get me.

I heard people calling, "Medic! Medic!" I could look around a little bit and I saw to the left, my best buddy dying of shrapnel. He was hit from mortar shrapnel that got him in the hip. I could see the blood oozing out. He was glassy eyed. He was about ten feet from me, and I knew he was a goner and nothing could be done for him. It just broke my heart. I was awful glad I was still in one piece, but it was a mess. And to my right there was the captain lying there, and his one leg was blown off at the knee; it just looked like it was held together by a little strip of skin. No bones just a little strip of skin was holding his leg to the rest of his body, and he was moaning and really in bad shape. And I don't know what happened to my sergeant. I never saw him again. I don't know whether he survived or what. I don't know how many more were wounded or killed. Just didn't hear anything about them. It was chaos.

But finally our first sergeant came along and ordered the rest of us to leave everything like it is and advance farther into the woods where the rest of the soldiers were gathering and try to set up a defensive position. That's the last I saw of my friend Larry. We'd been bunk mates in England for a month. Poor guy died of loss of blood, I guess, from the shrapnel.

Finally I know some medics got to the captain to stop the blood from oozing out and gave him some morphine for the awful pain. They made him a stretcher. We learned it in basic training. You cut off branches with a knife or a hatchet and get some straight branches that are seven feet long and take an overcoat and put it buttons-down on the ground and pull the sleeves up and run the sleeves through the holes on the other side, and now if you lift it up, you've got a stretcher of sorts.

They came by me and I took a turn carrying the captain on this makeshift stretcher, and I could see that his face was totally grey. No blood showed at all in his face. His eyes were closed and he was unconscious at this point. But he was in terrible shape. I walked for some while before I let someone else take my place and that's the last I saw of the captain. I carried him to where the main area of the troops were. We were taking shelter in a circle on a low ridge as the best place to hold off the Germans, but it was totally impossible because they totally overwhelmed us like five to one, and they had artillery.

They left the captain at the side of the road. I heard later that when he got hit so bad, he was in such terrible pain and he knew he wasn't going to make it, he told the bystanders to shoot him and then mail his wallet to his wife. And they never did shoot him of course but, I learned later that he died that day.

It was awful. Awful.

Finally we were moved into a larger area where the rest of the crowd was trying to gather. Hours went by, and the Germans were wheeling up their artillery. We were hopelessly outgunned. The war had gone on behind us. We were trapped. The Germans not only surrounded us, but they were pouring westward to what became a big bulge in our lines, sixty-five miles deep. That is the Battle of the

Bulge. It was the bulge that the Germans made in the American lines.

The company of 160 or so men was now under command of the executive officer, Lt. Jack Stein. He had us again form a big circle of slit trenches in the woods to be a defensive position. We expected the Germans would come charging up that hill after us. We had left the field of battle trying to capture Schönberg, but they were in the meantime wheeling up artillery to us and were going to wipe us out if they could.

We spent the morning and the rest of the afternoon, and I noticed that our regimental commander had his command post in a little slit trench about maybe fifty or sixty feet from where I was. Off to the side were laid out on the snow all of the wounded men that they had been able to bring in from wherever. I didn't see any medic doing anything about it. They could have been dead for all I know. They were just row on row lying there in the snow. Face up. But no one tending to any of them that I could see.

Hours went by, and I'm still digging my little slit trench, and it turns out I could see maybe fifty feet away the regimental commander with some of his junior officers looking very grave and grim. They seemed to be talking the situation over now. What was the best bet. Nothing much was happening. I found out later that our colonel asked for a volunteer from one of our officers to take over a flag of truce. The volunteer used a white undershirt or something tied to the top of a rifle like a white flag to see what he could find out about what terms if any the Germans wanted from us.

In due course, the volunteer came back and again I was twenty or thirty feet from where from where they were all gathered talking about it all. The colonel finally realized that it was hopeless. The war had gone on beyond us. The Germans had a huge force staying behind to take care of us who were trapped behind.

The terms were this: You surrender all, or we turn our artillery on you all and kill you. That was their threat. Whether they were really going to do it, who knows? They could have. They did it many times during the war. It was a very believable threat, so the colonel very correctly decided that our situation was hopeless. All we would do is get ourselves killed and not help the war. The war has gone past us.

The Germans came up, maybe ten men with submachine guns. looking over the group. One guy was like twenty feet from me. They had the white flag, and there were the rules of war that we were trying to obey. But I was so mad and I had my carbine and could've killed him with no trouble at all in vengeance for what he did to my friend. He was dying or already dead, and others were all blown up. I realized that was totally foolish because I would be breaking the normal rules of war, such as they were, and they would slaughter us all for sure because I had killed one of their men. They would be so angry, they would kill us all, and I thought that maybe one of my lieutenants would shoot me because they'd want to show the Germans, "We didn't really mean it. This guy was an idiot."

Those were the thoughts that were running through my mind. I still had my carbine, and I was a crack shot at it and I knew I could kill the first soldier I could see. I couldn't quite see how many there were there. I could have easily killed that German, no trouble, but I would bring the wrath of the whole German unit on our group. I would be causing the killing of all these men. Slaughter.

Slaughter. I wanted to have my own vengeance. I got my senses back and realized I couldn't possibly do this.

The Germans left. The second in command was now in charge of our company. Because the captain was dying, the first lieutenant automatically became the commander. We had about 160 men before all our casualties, of course, but he started making the rounds from slit trench area to slit trench. The Germans had said if we didn't surrender in like two hours they would move their artillery up and kill us all, not let anybody survive. We were just a problem for them to get rid of.

Our commander said we were going to try to stall them, but he said, "In the meantime, if anybody wants to slip away, it's still light time in Belgium. Feel free to take off. I suggest if you are going to take off go ten miles into the German lines and then north and finally west again to try to connect to our own troops."

I thought to myself that is the most idiotic thing to go where they are already bringing up more troops, more soldiers, guns. No way are you going to get through there. You are going to meet Germans. I don't know if anybody took advantage of that idea. I certainly didn't give it any thought. Nobody I knew did either.

Finally, he came back and told us to surrender at like five P.M. He said break up all your weapons and surrender by order of the colonel. He's the one that made this decision not me.

The colonel came to this conclusion. Why should we be slaughtered? We were in no way to help the war. The Germans had already proceeded to the west. Sixty-five miles into our lines, killing everybody in sight. We were a big pocket of nuisance to the Germans. They wanted to get rid of this pocket. They didn't mind if we surrendered, but they were going to get rid of this pocket or slaughter us all. I knew the Germans. They would slaughter us all if they thought it was militarily proper.

So I went back to my slit trench and I thought, "What am I going to do now?" I looked around and everyone around me was starting to break up their weapons. A corporal standing next to me had a pistol, not a powerful rifle, and he was foolishly getting rid of his ammunition. He was an idiot that didn't get trained very well. He forgot there was one bullet left in the magazine, and you have to take it out of the handle. He had cocked it, and there was one bullet left in the chamber. So as he put it down to his side he decided to click it to make sure it was empty. He shot his own leg. That was ridiculous.

So finally the German soldiers appeared, and all that remained was for us to break up our weapons and have the Germans take control of us. I felt so helpless and enraged and so miserably cold and wondering what the Germans were going to do with us once we surrendered.

I destroyed my beloved carbine. You could disassemble it to some extent. Threw all my bullets in the snow. I put the carbine against a tree and with my boot I broke it by busting the stock near the trigger mechanism, and I threw both pieces in the snow somewhere. I felt like a trapped rat. Waiting to be put who knows where. I didn't know whether they would just kill us all or what they would do. Well, thanks very much, and I didn't get a cigar for winning the war.

After going through this hell, seeing my friends being killed by my side even, at the moment I wasn't thinking anything of the future. I didn't think I would live another day. Later on I would say, when I had peace and quiet and even years to think about it, I first thank my lucky stars and my creator that I was allowed to live through this terrible battle.

I remember thinking at the time during my training in the states that I realize I'm in the infantry, which takes most of the casualties, and someday I might be killed or maimed or something, but the thought of being taken prisoner hardly if ever crossed my mind. That seemed to be highly unlikely thing to happen to a soldier, but it happened to us.

P.O.W.

It was hopeless. I realized that all I could do was wait for the Germans to show up and take us prisoner. The Germans started coming in by foot and finally by truck and right into our midst. They were singing and shouting songs of victory and so forth and to me they looked half drunk, but it was the first time in a long time that the Germans had a big victory.

I was amazed that they lined us up. They separated the officers and put them under special heavier guard. I remember how sharp they were. Particularly how they had lined up their artillery pieces wheel to wheel up the hill, ready to kill us all if we had not surrendered. They were capable of doing this, as you know, if you knew anything about the war. That sort of thing happened a lot.

We made our way down. They were searching us for cigarettes, watches, any weapons, and I had one minor victory. I had a cheap Westclox wristwatch that I carried all through training. It was probably worth about fifteen bucks in today's money when I bought it, but I had what was called then a watch pocket in the upper right part of my pants next to where the belt went by. It was a little slit pocket designed just for watches, and that's what I did: I took my watch off my wrist, folded up the leather band, and stuck it into the watch pocket.

The Germans came by and grabbed my wrists and looked inside my jacket and all that for a box of cigarettes that was popular for them and any weapons and gave me a shove to get back down the line with the rest of them. When I finally got home from the war, I still had that watch and I kept it for a souvenir for a long time. When my son David came along, when he was like three or four years old, I gave it to him as a little toy to play with. It soon vanished but I thought well that's okay. At least I lived long enough to give it to my son.

We had a long walk, and I remember passing where a battle had taken place. I saw a German soldier lying face down halfway over a barbed wire, which had been strung by the Germans or the Americans I don't know which, and he was obviously dead.

It was so miserable at times, and I felt such a sense of despair about what's going to become of me and the rest of our guys and oh what do we do. And what will they do to us?

I remember vividly walking alongside of a guy as we were walking. We were walking four abreast, and the guards were walking on the outside of the group of four or five, and they were spaced like every fifty feet. I looked to the right and I discovered that the man walking to my right was an officer. He was a young man, and I could see the gold stripe and the gold pin of a second lieutenant, but he was wearing a GI enlisted man's overcoat. Somehow he'd escaped being identified as an officer, but he had grabbed a coat maybe from a dead soldier. He was disguised as an enlisted man, so I think he thought he had a better chance of escaping with a large group of men rather than a heavily guarded group of officers.

I could see he was very tense and nervous. I was talking to him and he wasn't talking to me and he was very nervous trudging along. I could see his eyes flashing with adrenaline. He was ready to do something. It turned out we were making a right turn around curve of a hill. It was all kind of wooded there, and up on the top of the hill we were momentarily out of the sight of guards, and at that instant he burst up the hill. He didn't say anything to me or anything at all. He just started running up the hill. Of course guys like myself starting hissing, "Don't look. Don't look." And everyone turned their heads away, waiting to hear a shot from a rifle or a pistol.

We heard nothing. We kept walking in the dark. It was pitch dark at this point. Walking in the dark. I always wondered what happened to that officer who tried his best to escape. Chances are he didn't get far, given the situation. The place was crawling with Germans. My best guess is that he was either killed or captured soon after he left our group. I'll never know. His story never appeared in all the magazines that I've been getting for years.

They finally let us sleep on the ground in a German town called Prüm. Now we were heading east back further into Germany. There was a church there. It was either a Lutheran or Catholic church from the looks of it. Some of us sneaked into the church, where it was at least warmer than outside in the snow. Everybody else was sleeping out and trying to sleep lying down in the snow and, like myself, didn't have anything to lie on except my clothes I had to walk around in.

So some of us slipped into this church and tried to lie down on the pews near the back. We were there for about two minutes and in comes a German with a rifle, and he says, "Raus, raus." We understood from his gestures that "Raus" meant "Get out of here and go back to where you came from." It would have been nice if they'd let us all sleep in the church overnight, but they didn't. They insisted we get out.

I didn't want to lie in the snow. I stood all night long watching the artillery battle going on further away. Frozen to the bone. That's how I had my feet and my hands frozen all the way on my way to the prison camp. And the next day we marched all day long. We slept that night after marching all the next day further to the east, and we finally got to a town called Gerolstein, and we were allowed to sleep in a large barn and storehouse, but still had no food. That was a big improvement. There was no heat but no wind blowing. It was bitter cold. I remember I tried to take my boots off so I could rub my feet, and I could see the laces and my skin started to bulge out from my shoe. I thought, "Oh man, if I take these shoes off, my feet will be twice the size they normally are and I'll never get my shoes back on. I have to have my shoes to survive." So I tied my shoes as tight as I could and that was that.

The next day I discovered there was a train track nearby, and they got us in groups and loaded us into boxcars. These boxcars were smaller than the boxcars we know of today in the United States. They were shorter, and they were used in World War I for transportation by armies on all sides. They called them "forty-and-eights" in those days: forty men or eight horses was the capacity of each car.

They counted us off and loaded us sixty men per car. Exactly sixty.

I was somehow separated from the other guys of my twelve-man squad. I never saw any of my squad members again. It was really tough. Some of the walking wounded were allowed to stretch out in the middle of the car floor. There was no stove, no heat of any kind, just the warmth given out by our bodies. I remember I was able to sit against the side of the wall of the car, and some guys just had to sit on the floor with nothing to rest their knees against except maybe the knees of the guy next to them. All together we spent eight days and nights in that boxcar.

I remember sitting there in total shock and I kept thinking to myself and the other soldiers, now prisoners, were now pretty much thinking the same thing: How could we ever have gotten into such a terrible mess? I had never really ever thought of the idea of being a prisoner, as I had mentioned before, and here I was now cold, miserable, frozen feet, frozen hands, and wondering what was going to become of me and the rest of us.

I know we, at least thinking for myself, thought how could I have done so badly for our division? But the rational explanation, which was true, was that we were put in a very bad position. We were not able to mount any kind of a defense strung out over miles of territory. But we were finally all brought together, I read after the war, about seven thousand of us altogether out of fourteen thousand were captured. In addition to that, hundreds were killed and many more than that wounded.

I just wondered, how did we ever get in this mess? It took me a lot of thinking for months and months and even years to sort it all out. But anyway, finally the train started up and started moving ahead, and I discovered along the way that the car in front of our car was filled with German guards. I'm pretty sure they were pretty comfortable. They didn't have sixty in their car. Every time the train would stop for any reason, for the guards and not for us, they would get out of their car and take up positions along the tracks to make sure no one was busting out of a car one way or another. It was virtually impossible but you never know. When the train was going to start again, they would all get back into the car in front of me. I don't know if there were other cars with German guards in it, but I do know of seeing them over the eight days from time to time, there was at least a carload of German guards riding in front of us.

But when I was in my freight car, I never heard a sound of the car in front of me or any human voices, just the voices of us guys in our car. Anyway it wasn't as miserable cold anymore but cold enough.

We finally crossed the river at this town called Koblenz, which was at a bridge over the Rhine River, a very wide river running north to south, a natural fortification for the Germans to fall back behind, which they did.

It was the evening of the twenty-third of December. We were captured on the nineteenth and we got in the boxcars on the midday on the twenty-first of December. The twenty-third was two days be-

George's POW ID photo taken by his German captors

fore Christmas. We were well aware of that. We were all wondering what was going on at home. My, oh my.

Do my parents know I'm still alive? Do they know I've been in a battle? Do they know if I've been wounded or anything? I didn't know the answer to those questions, and I wouldn't know the answers for about five months. It was just gnawing at me the whole time I was in the prison camp, not knowing whether my parents knew and how they were taking it. Was it affecting their health and so on? It was pretty miserable.

Anyway on the evening of December twenty-third, it was already dark and it was already winter in Germany. It got dark at four-thirty or five o'clock, something like that, and we were sitting in this coal-black car. I was sitting up against the wall and we were all sitting there quietly and probably all thinking of home and family and all that and whatever else was on our mind. One of the soldiers near the front of the car, I could tell from the sound of his voice, started singing Christmas songs. I'm sure it was to cheer us all up, including himself. He had a very nice voice. I'm sure he had sung in a choir because I had sung in a choir myself in high school, and I knew a good voice when I heard one. And his was very good.

And finally he was singing, "Silent night, Holy night, all is calm, All is bright. . . ." As he was singing we all saw a very bright red light shining through a little window in the box cars, and we were trying to figure out what does that bright light mean? Well it turned out to be flares dropped by British Pathfinder planes, which had down-looking radar, and the weather, which had been miserable up until the twenty-third of December, had finally cleared.

No planes of any kind had been flying in our defense of German attack, and now all of a sudden the Pathfinder plane had been looking at the train yard that we happened to be parked in at that time. We were on the northern edge of it as I found out later.

We had just about figured out that that flare meant no good. All of a sudden we started hearing deafening explosions and brilliant lights accompanied by each explosion. It turned out that the British Pathfinder plane, which was a fighter plane in size, found that he was looking for this train yard. This was his target for the night. The British were bombing the train yard so the Germans couldn't bring more soldiers up or supplies or ammunition, military, or prisoners of war.

Later I found out it turned out to be bombs raining on us and near us and on a nearby prisoner of war camp, and we had stopped there because the Germans thought they were going to take all of us prisoners off there and go the prison camp. It turned out that the prison camp was already filled by the time our train had got there, and they were going to move us on, and then the bombing started.

We were all yelling trying to get out of this car, and we figured it was likely to get blown up by the bombs, and somehow or other the sliding door slid open and out we poured. Some guys ran up a sloping hill. Most of the guys with me were running alongside of the train trying to keep the shelter of the train between us and any bombs falling by, not to get up on a high ridge. So we were running alongside of the train, and it was still being emptied of prisoners getting down, and one of the Germans opened the door.

One of the GIs, who happened to be a really skinny guy, climbed out one of those windows after tearing out the barbed wire that covered the windows, which was ten inches high and two feet wide or something. No glass for fresh air, just barbed wire nailed in place. Somehow they were able to rip off the barbed wire, and this guy skittled out the window and opened the doors for his car, which were not padlocked, just covered with wire wrapped through the hasps because the Germans didn't have padlocks to spare to fool with something like that. All they did was put wire through where the two rings would slide together. Of course the wire was strong, and you couldn't slide the door open from inside.

Anyway we were all helping open other doors, and we eventually all got out. I found myself running down the side of the train. I found myself at a tool shed. This was one building about five feet high and eight feet square, and there was a door on it. Some guys were running into the wooden shack for shelter from the bombs, and someone yelled, "Don't get in there, that would be a target for the bombs!" It was an idiotic thing to say, because if a bomb hit anywhere near that shed it would be splintered into kindling wood and anyone inside of it would be killed just as easily standing outside of it as standing in it. But that's how the mind doesn't work right at times. I continued running, and I found myself running into a sloping hill and what turned out to be a quarry, which is a hole in the ground about fifty feet down or so. I got to the bottom of it, and I found there were horizontal tunnels leaning into the side of the hill where they were apparently mining certain kinds of rock or something.

I pushed my way into this tunnel already filled with GIs and a German guard was also in the tunnel. The guys in the back said, "There's no more room in here, stay out," and we said, "We're coming in!" We all shoved our way in.

We all waited out all of these terrific explosions with like five-hundred-pound bombs with a blinding light and a concussion that would make everything shake nearby. And finally after what seemed like an eternity, the bombing stopped, the planes stopped and were on their way. It turned out from pictures I saw later that they had really destroyed the rail yard, but the car that I was on and most of the others were not damaged. There was one hole high up on one side of our car made by some sort of flying debris or shrapnel or whatever it was, but other than that the car was okay.

If we had stayed in the car, we would have been free of danger it turned out. Ha. Ha.

But anyway, the guard finally started shouting, "Raus, raus," and beckoning with his bayonet and rifle, and we made our way out of the tunnel and back to the train. We got to the top of the quarry and saw dead men and wounded men lying all over the place, and it was really terrible.

I remember another GI ran up to me and wanted my first aid kit, which everybody had on their belts and contained a bandage and some sulfa powder and I presume not much else, but at least something to make a tourniquet or save somebody's life possibly. A soldier said, "Give me your first aid kit," and I didn't want to give it to him at first, I might need it for myself because who knows where the next bomb was going to drop somewhere, but I reluctantly gave it up to him. I had to. There was nothing else I could do, and he ran off to this wounded guy and helped bandage him up.

We finally got back to our boxcars and there were seven or eight guys missing from the count. We stood outside waiting to be counted, and they finally got us all back in the car together again.

They slammed it shut. I'm sure they wired it again, and there we were in the dark again. Miserable. Wondering what the heck hit us; at that point in time we didn't know it was British bombers. I found out all of that later.

Somebody from the back of the car said to the guy who was sitting in the front of the car, "Hey guy, how about singing some more songs to cheer us up?" and there was no response. And we thought about it, and we realized that one of those bodies lying out there was this poor guy who didn't know at the time he was singing his own funeral service when he was singing to cheer us up.

That was one of the darkest days of my life that I can recall. I'll never forget that. I think about this poor guy. The last thing he was doing was cheering up his fellow prisoners. He gave his life to the bombs that fell. He must have been one of those men who went running up hill instead of running a lower profile. I do remember a bomb falling from that hill and a brilliant light explosion, and I looked back and I could see a blinding light, and it's probably at that point when all those men were killed.

The next day was Christmas Eve day, and I looked out a little crack in the side of the door. I made my way up to the front where the sliding door was and looked through a broken bullet hole. I could see just a little bit through, and I could see horse-drawn wagons dragging the dead bodies onto these farmer wagons on the way. They were taking overcoats off the dead bodies before they put the bodies in the wagons.

Later in the day they brought wagons loaded with loaves of bread and gave a number of loaves for each car. I think there was about one loaf for about every seven or eight prisoners. It was heavy rye bread. It wasn't very tasty at all, but later we got used to it.

They also brought some Red Cross parcels to share. They were eleven-pound parcels, I later found out, that the International Red Cross had provided by way of the American Red Cross, the Canadian Red Cross, and the English Red Cross, and once in a while in the months that would pass I would get to share a box with another prisoner.

Eventually we arrived at a prisoner of war camp, Stalag IV-B, near Mühlberg. After a few weeks, we were transferred; thirty-five of us were put on a train and taken far, far into Germany to the Polish border and put to work in a German factory weaving blankets on a weaving machine under guard. A German woman was in charge of supervising our prison labor at the blanket factory. She taught me how to make blankets on a machine and we consistently broke the materials and machines. We were still bugging the lady with the broken threads and all; that was our only amusement and morale builder we had during that time.

We were losing weight and once in a while we would share one of the eleven-pound Red Cross food parcels prepared in England, United States, or Canada. Those parcels were life savers. They contained items like powered milk, a can of corned beef, a can of cheese, a chocolate bar, a pack of cigarettes, tea leaves. Whenever these parcels arrived, like once a month, we would share it with two men.

Occasionally the German guards would take a couple of us guys or we would volunteer to go under guard to another place in the town. We were held in this locked barn with a big padlock in front overnight when we weren't working. We were locked in this little prison.

Everyday some of us were taken to another location under guard to pick up some food to eat. They had a kitchen there they were building. They had other prisoners there including women prisoners who were doing some cooking and whatnot. They cooked some soup for us, and we'd carry these big cans back to our own prison.

This one time I was sitting on a bench waiting for the food to be prepared for us to lug back to our camp, and an old German guard, who was probably a little bit forgetful to say the least, on easy duty guarding us, put his rifle down next to me. He started chit-chatting with the cooks about giving him an extra bowl of soup, and just then the rifle fell to the floor. He didn't park it exactly right against the wall.

The loaded rifle was sitting next to me, and then it fell over, and the old German heard it fall, and he came over to get the rifle. I got up from my little bench and I picked it up from the floor. He came over to me, and he was very embarrassed and shocked because he would have been severely reprimanded by his officers if they had found out he had done such a dumb thing with a prisoner—even though it was hopeless for me to do anything with the rifle. Here I was about a thousand miles from the American lines. How would I get there? How would I eat on the way there? How would I escape being captured by guards at bridges? Where would I sleep? It was hopelessly ridiculous trying to escape under those conditions.

I picked up the rifle. He didn't know what I was going to do with it. He didn't know if I was going to shoot him. I grabbed the stock and handed it to him sideways, vertical. It wasn't pointed at him. He sighed a big sigh of relief and went back to mumbling to himself, very embarrassed at what he had done.

I would have been shot by people looking for people escaping. I would have been one guy with one rifle with say six shots in it against say ten guys coming at me with their guns. I didn't like the odds of getting out with a loaded rifle in my possession. So that wasn't going to work.

At the blanket factory, we were hungry a lot. Daydreaming about food. But we also realized that we were lucky in a way because we weren't doing really hard labor somewhere, let's say working in cement. And we also realized while we were hungry and under guard and under arrest with a very uncertain future, other British and American men were dying on the battlefield far away. Here we were high and dry but with a very uncertain future. We worried whether we'd be killed in a battle between the Germans and the Russians.

The Russians were coming. We knew that. They were now in Poland and coming quickly. The Germans had already been beaten back by the Russians. We found out all of this by various methods. We also found out that the Americans had already restored the front to where it was before the Battle of the Bulge, and they were advancing toward the Rhine River, the last big barrier to overcoming Germany. And the Russians were coming from the east.

I personally worried whether the Germans would simply have us all executed rather than allow us to be liberated. Or what would the Russians do if the Russians got there first? Would they send us to a Russian gulag? Or kill us?

We were just pawns being used by others. I remember one of my worst fears was what was happening to my parents and my sisters and brothers. I didn't know whether they knew I was alive or not, or if I was suffering from grievous wounds. I had no way to find out because there was no such thing as incoming mail or newspapers. All we heard was German propaganda from time to time, but we could read between the lines.

I found out after the war, it was four months after I was captured that mail arrived from me from Germany. Up to that time, my parents were only told by telegram that their son was missing in action. Later they heard that there were no reports from any source, the International Red Cross or the Germans, that I was dead. It was assumed that I was missing in action and probably a prisoner, but they got no further word about that until I was liberated. It was tough mentally wondering what my parents were thinking.

Little did I know that my older brother Bob was already in Europe. I left the States before he did. It turned out, he left about a month later and saw a lot of action in the 69th Division.

It was barely February, 1945 that we started hearing thunderous artillery off to the east. That would have been the Russians. The German Army was combatting them. The sounds were coming closer and closer over a day or so. Finally, all the artillery stopped. We didn't know whether the Russians had retreated, the Germans had retreated, or what, but things were getting hot and heavy to the east.

In mid-February, the guards came into the hut where we lived in the evening and rousted us all out and led us to the basement of a nearby bakery to be used as a bomb shelter. They didn't tell us what was going on besides bombing, but we could see out of the base of the building a great fire burning off to the west.

We knew something terrible was going on somewhere. After many hours, the sky was lit from one end to the other with fire and this was like thirty miles away. We were finally led back to our huts and to our cots and we went to sleep wondering what had happened.

A city we had passed through had never been bombed before. That was the target we were watching burning from thirty miles away, and bombing continued the next day during daylight. It was the British who bombed that at nighttime, and, we found out later during the war, the American Air Force. (There was no separate Air Force in World War II; the planes and the gunners and all that were part of the Army. There was no distinction there. A few years after the war, they made a separate branch for the Air Force.)

We were wondering what became of all those people we saw there, and I remember thinking that there are thousands of more or less innocent people who were blown to bits or burned to death. It was a fire raging for miles in every direction. I just couldn't contemplate.

I thought to myself, "My gosh, the destruction must have been enormous because it came without any warning. These poor devils that were there were burned to death or suffocated by a lack of oxygen or burning bombs or blown to pieces. There was a huge, huge destruction."

I remember the next morning the guards came into the building and said,

"Dresden ist kaput."

Meaning Dresden is dead.

A different way of killing people; the war sure came into Dresden. I learned after the war, that more people were killed there, believe it or not, then were killed in Hiroshima. We really felt guilty and yet happy that the war was coming closer and closer to a finish. That we could all survive and go home.

A few days later, a bunch of us were taken to a building where we had never been before, and some German civilians had us unload from the attic bundles and bundles of bandages that the Ladies' Aid Society had spent the whole war making. They were made out of crepe paper like you would use for decorating a party room, not cloth, paper made by a machine of the type that made those streamers that we were used to in the States.

They took us to a local small hospital building, a single-story building about a block long, where they were bringing the wounded soldiers. Our job was to dig a deep trench to bring the patients into if the town was bombed. We spent weeks digging this six-foot-deep trench with just picks and shovels. Still lousy food every day, but we did that for weeks.

One time we were taking a little break under guard, and along came a strange caravan: horse-drawn wagons were filled with "German" soldiers with "German" rifles and uniforms, but they were Russian. They had been captured and decided that they wanted to fight on the German side because they hated the Russian Communist rulers.

I stood in awe as several horse-drawn wagons trudged along. I remember there wasn't any expression on their faces. They were swarthy-looking men. Cossacks. We just wondered what their future would be, I remember. They had no future. When they were finally captured, they would surely be executed.

I remember this one time of complaining of a toothache to our guards. I hadn't had a toothbrush for five months while I was a prisoner, and it was hurting me a lot. The guards, knowing that the war was going to be ending soon, were starting to treat us in a more or less civil way without a lot of shouting, and I made clear, by way of this American who spoke German, that I was in pain. They arranged to take me to a local civilian dentist's office under guard, and I remember being taken there by a beautiful blonde girl. She was maybe eighteen, my age, but when she saw me, she turned on the most vicious, hateful look at me.

I thought, "Wow, man, she hates all Americans." I couldn't blame her, from her point of view frankly. She just burned a hole through me with hatred. And I thought I wonder what is going to happen to this girl when the Russians or the Americans arrive. In the meantime, the German dentist patched up my tooth and on my way I went.

So the war struck people in strange ways. With the Hitler Youth, this beautiful girl, it was just weird and strange. The Germans I knew were going to reap the results of the way they treated the Russians, particularly early in the war. They were executing Russians wholesale when they captured them and so forth, and this was well known back home.

I wondered what would become of that beautiful blonde girl when the Russians got ahold of her. I don't know if she would live through that experience, and I know that after the war there was an awful lot of raping and killing being done by the Russians in payment of all that had been done to them.

I remember another day in the prison camp, one of the guards, a younger man (I suspect the younger ones had all been declared unfit for further combat fighting because of wounds they had suffered) was in charge of keeping track of all us coming and going through the truck. At one point he lost count, and he was worried that some of us had escaped. I'm sure he knew he'd be punished severely if any of us escaped under his watch.

I happened to be standing there, and he pulled out his pistol and he pointed his pistol at us and yelling in German. One of the guys who was with me was the other one who also spoke German. I was watching his feet and I didn't move. I didn't breathe! Because the guard was so nervous, he had his finger on the trigger, and if somebody as much moved their arm, he would start shooting. He was only about three feet away from us. He really went berserk.

One of us Americans could speak German. He spoke up to the German guard and calmed him down and said, "Now, now where would we go? There's no place to go. Nobody escaped. There's no problem. Take another count." And the guard calmed down, and I thought, "Wow a prisoner never knows what's going to happen next."

I learned a little German from listening to our German guards yelling at us. Once I said in German to the guard, "That horse looks like it's ready for the glue factory."

We found out that the German Army was being pushed back by the Russian Army. The little town where we lived was being transformed into a defensive position. They started building very high log walls around the edge of the village, not far from where our hut was. They had the Hitler Youth smartly dressed in their uniforms carrying picks and shovels over their shoulders, singing songs in German. You know, patriotic songs of some sort. Totally brainwashed and ready to go off to wherever.

When we returned to our prison the next day, we discovered that the Hitler Youth had dug a trench suitable for putting in an artillery piece right next to our building, aiming in the direction of the big door they had built out of logs leading to the back end at the end of the village. We realized that we were now going to live next door to where they were putting an artillery piece as defense for when the Russians come. The thought was so futile and so insane that by this time the Germans all knew that they were losing the war, but they were still following orders.

STALAG IV-B

We returned to Stalag IV-B from our stint at the blanket factory. It was amazing to be back in the confines of that huge concentration camp, though it wasn't a concentration camp, it was a prisoner of war camp. My first confinement there was only for about two weeks, and as it turned out, I was going to be there for about five weeks shortly before the end of the war. I'll begin by saying here I was back at the old place and to my amazement my buddy Larkin Mayfield and myself were assigned to the same barracks building that I had been in my first time around since I had been in the blanket factory. This time there were no bunks available, and no one volunteered any space.

I remember that there was a homemade table that the prisoners had made over the years, and we used it to eat our meals at. It was about as big as a dining room table, and but it was more narrow than the one I had at home. At any rate Mayfield and I got permission from the barracks leader to sleep on top of that table, even though there was no mattress or padding of any kind, but it sure beat sleeping out of doors, which was what we had done early in the battles. Each of us still had an overcoat. It was late March, so we used one overcoat as a mattress on top of this rough-hewn table and the other coat as the blanket.

We slept in the clothes we were wearing because they were the only clothes we had. Twenty-four hours a day, day after day we were in the same clothes. We found there was a water spigot and wash basin attached to our hut—-actually it was two huts separated by a washroom—and everyone shared it. Hundreds of men shared it. One basin and a cold water spigot.

I was able to clean my body more or less, and by that time I had a razor and I could shave. I don't know if I had soap or not but I did shave, but I didn't have a toothbrush. I didn't have a toothbrush for five months. I remember that very well. So I'd have a sort of bird bath every day, and every once in a while, kind of wash my clothes after a fashion. It was still messy, and I never felt really clean.

The Brits were non-commissioned airmen. We Americans like Larkin and myself were like street bums or derelicts rather than soldiers, whereas these men had been prisoners for several years. Earlier on they were able to get resupplied with decent uniforms and whatnot, but we had nothing like that.

I looked around after getting acquainted with the place again, and I found that the place really hadn't changed any after I had left. The Polish doctor told me that things had gotten worse, but to me it wasn't apparent. It was the same old miserable, highly guarded place that it had been before.

The weather was now more calm and nice and even pleasant some days, and I struck up a friendship with an English sergeant who had been a gunner who bailed out of a plane. We would take daily walks around the compound. He was very intelligent, and I would ask him questions on what it was like back in England and so forth before the war and told him about the month I spent there.

He was very soft spoken, and I discovered he had a hand-washing phobia. Every time he would leave me, he would say well I'm going over to wash my hands, and I had the feeling he was afraid of catching something from me. This derelict-looking character and that's why he was always washing his hands after we would part. I couldn't blame him. After the war I remember trying to reach him, and no one seemed to remember him among the British people I had contacted by letter. But I'm sure he got home safely.

One day I remember the British, who really ran the camp because they really could speak English (but they took their directions from the Germans of course who were ever–present), announced that they were looking for volunteers for a work party to Leipzig, Germany, which was further west more toward where the Americans were coming from. They were saying that it was meant to be a pick-and-shovel job, cleaning up the mess from the bombing of Leipzig and removing dead bodies and stuff like that. I didn't like the idea at all of being in a big city where it was still being subject to bombing, when out at the camp, we were really in the farm country. The town of Lehrberg was so little it was of no military consequence.

I decided that the job wasn't for me. I'd rather take my chances where I was. I didn't know what was going to be happening, but we knew that the British and American armies were coming from the west and a lot of terrible battles were going on, and the same from the Russians coming from the east meeting where we were. When the British guys were having a little assembly, I slipped around the other way on the side of building and hid there until they broke up the formation. And I guess they got enough volunteers to go to Leipzig.

Every day it was something different, and the ever-present watchtowers were there and they had a dead line wire: The guard posts were up in the towers every three-hundred feet or so, and double barbed wire on the outside around the perimeter, and then there was a small wire only about two-feet high on little wooden sticks about twenty feet away from the real barbed wire. This was just an ordinary wire. Not barbed wire, just one strand and the whole deal.

You dared not cross pass the one wire toward the fence. If you did, the machine gunners and the riflemen in the towers would open fire on you.

I remember that, when going on my walks with this British guy, we would be careful. We would be walking near that little two-foot-high fence once in a while, but we would be very careful not to make any moves like we were going to take a dash across the fence.

We made our way around, and he was good company. He didn't say too much of any consequence but he was open to conversation. It was nice to get fresh air and get out in the open again and not freeze to death like I did in the winter time. But I remember in April, word spread through the camp that Franklin Roosevelt had died the day before. It was sad and unhappy news to the British and the Americans. We were very sad because we recognized that Winston Churchill and England and Franklin Roosevelt and America were really the heart and soul of planning the now near end of the war.

I remember the British compound turned out with all their nice uniforms and put on a nice majestic parade in honor of President Roosevelt, and we Americans stood around the perimeter watching. These British soldiers had marched with great precision and made a rectangular cycle all around the open area. I was very impressed and yet kind of embarrassed that we Americans didn't do anything about it. The Brits had better uniforms and so forth and put on a very nice, moving memorial service. I don't remember if anybody spoke or not, I forget. That was really a stunning day to honor President Roosevelt, and we felt victory was in sight.

Every evening was something new we didn't have the last time I was at Stalag IV-B: The British had managed to assemble at least one secret radio, and they had brought in radio tubes in parts, and they had a way of hiding the radio from occasional barracks searches. At say eight o'clock at night, well after dark, a man would show up who was not a member of our barracks. He was the official messenger, and he would read a summary of the day's war news and everyone waited in great anticipation of it. So finally every evening we would get a news cast. The messenger wrote it all out, and I think he would go from barracks to barracks. We realized by now that what we thought was happening was in fact happening. The German Army was being overrun in the west, and the Russian forces were overrunning the German forces in the east.

It was a very interesting time. Of course I was still losing weight, and I didn't have to work anymore. I just passed the day wandering around. I was sitting around talking to people. Waiting for the next bucket of food to come around in the morning or whenever it was.

This was now the middle of April, a few days after the memorial service for President Franklin Roosevelt, and I volunteered for a work party to go into the town of Mühlberg. I think it was about three miles away. The job involved pushing a heavy hay wagon with a rig that could be hooked up to a couple of horses, but we were going to be the horses pushing this thing to go to a railroad depot to pick up some Red Cross parcels.

I happily volunteered to go because it was a glorious thing to do to bring back a load of Red Cross food parcels. This was very good news because we were all very thin and losing weight by the day. Along the way, we were pushing this wagon and I was a tiller; I held the front part of that long pole that the horses would normally be hooked to, which would turn the wheels to left or right or straight. In effect I was the steerer or helmsman, which meant I didn't have to do any pushing. My job was simply to keep it on the straight and narrow on this dirt road until we got to the town and the same thing on the way back.

But along the way, we could see German soldiers practicing in a big field not far from the road. There was a lot of shrubbery and trees, but through an opening we could see a whole bunch of German soldiers running around doing some maneuvers. There were large wooden targets painted to look like British or American tanks. And these men were being trained how to shoot an anti-tank rocket and aim properly while either running or walking or lying down. You had to be fairly close to your target because the range was only about maybe fifty yards, and it would fall to the ground whether you liked it or not.

We went on and got to the rail station and loaded up the wagon with a lot of parcels. We were all thrilled doing this job, and then on the way back, I was at the tiller again at the very front and aiming the front wheel of the wagon so the wagon is straight on the road while the rest of the guys are pushing the back and the side of the wagon.

As we were passing the training field, we heard machine gun fire going on, and we all turned and looked and saw a fighter plane strafing the field where the German soldiers had been training. As the plane zoomed by, I couldn't see whether it was an American plane or a Russian plane. That was the first instance of any combat where Stalag IV-B was.

Obviously, whoever it was had command of the skies there. When we got back to the camp, we told everybody what happened. The entire mood of the camp changed. What had only been a dream of particularly the British prisoners for two or three years that some-day maybe they'd be liberated, here was the day when the Allied fighter plane is shooting machine gun bullets at German soldiers. The whole mood of the camp changed from only a dream of liberation someday to days coming soon and it's for real.

It changed the whole mood of the lackadaisical prisoners, all the while worrying whether we would be killed by either attacks from the Russian troops or the American troops or executed by German guards as their vengeance. We didn't know. We realized that the war was now coming to our area.

Every morning thereafter, German fighter planes zoomed real low, two hundred feet above the camp heading from the north toward Berlin. We were about eighty miles away ourselves from Berlin. Later two Allied fighter planes would appear, and they started machine gunning any kind of target they could see of military value. When they finished up their ammunition, I guess, they didn't touch the camp and away they went to where they came from. It was really amazing. After they disappeared, that same German fighter plane would reappear coming from the east and go over our camp going back to where it had come from.

I speculated that the Allied mission was to destroy German planes so the German fighter pilot stayed out of range while the Allies were bombing. He was getting the plane out of harm's way because he knew they were strafing, and he would head back from where he had come from, so it was kind of getting interesting.

One day I heard a very loud explosion coming from the other end of camp and wondered what it was, so I decided to investigate. I ran into some British officers, and they pointed out the window in the back toward an open field and waved to a railroad track with a freight train on it a couple of city blocks away. The freight train wasn't moving, four or five cars were visible to me, but trees were blocking my view.

The last freight car was burning, and the British soldiers said the car behind had just blown up sky high. I waited and sure enough all of a sudden the last freight car went up in a tremendous explosion. It just disappeared into black with all the black dust and when the dust settled, there was no car there anymore but the car next to it was already on fire. I watched while the next car blew up. Finally there were no freight cars left. I figure the freight cars were full of ammunition or other explosives, and our planes were having a field day bombing those things.

So that's the way life went, and it was kind of entertainment going on there. I was usually by myself when I was watching, so I was always watching the sky and wondering what would be next. One day I saw two planes, which probably were American but maybe Russian, fly nearby. They were about three-quarters of a mile from the east where the Russians were coming from. I saw the first plane go into a steep dive going into a target. He was zooming down like a dive bomber, and as he was coming down, I could see something on the ground that was like a water tank or a facility, and as the plane was coming down I could see little puffs of explosions in the air—-anti-aircraft fire on the ground—-and the plane zoomed on and dropped the bombs down and away.

The second plane was following close by, and it was coming down the very same path when the other plane was hit by anti-aircraft fire, and I thought, "Wow he's a real daredevil, flying so fast at a forty-five-degree angle down." To me, it looked like the same path exactly and the same anti-aircraft exploding as he was coming closer, and there was a lot of smoke and little dark spots, which I am sure was shrapnel, and I couldn't hear any noise. But the plane came down and released its bomb, and as it pulled away, I could see smoke streaming out of the back of his plane. He was hit by the anti-aircraft fire, and I thought to myself, "Boy, I hope this guy makes it back somehow." These were very versatile planes, and they could go any which way they wanted. I felt sorry for the pilot. I don't know what ever happened to that plane. It was very exciting.

I was about five weeks at this camp at that point. One day a group of American and British men including myself were out on what we called the parade ground—-a big open space where everybody had been lined up by the barracks. We heard the loud drone of planes getting louder and louder, and as we looked up in the sky to the west, we could see there were B7 American bombers coming all in formation, and they were coming right in the direction of our camp. They weren't flying awful high because they weren't afraid of anti-aircraft fire in that vicinity.

They were heading right for our camp, and we thought, "My God we are all going to obliterated!" because they were coming right over us. They went over us at a forty-five-degree angle, and coming up at them we saw a flare come out of the front lead plane, and we thought, "Uh–oh, that's a marker," and that's where the plane drops the bombs. It was red flare and when the planes got to where the flare was, they made a right turn right before our eyes in a beautiful formation, and they started heading north up toward what was Tarnow, Germany, maybe fifteen miles north of us. We all heaved a collective sigh of relief that we were not going to be obliterated. At least today.

Every day was getting more exciting. Another morning some days later, I was standing around with some men in a hut just talking about what's happening and it can't be long before the Americans or the Russians on the ground, we think, and all of a sudden something like hail hit on the roof of our barracks. We all hit the ground and wondered what the heck happened. It only lasted a few seconds.

We looked around and realized that a fighter plane had gone past. The word finally passed around that the fighter plane mistook a party of prisoners on the road, who had been taken under guard to a nearby forest to gather branches of wood to be used in the kitchen buildings to get the hot soup that we get every morning, for a party of Germans. He came in at a very low angle, and he strafed some and killed some poor American prisoners. As he continued up, his bullets fired into the camp, and that's what we heard rattling on the roof of our camp. It was the bullets from this plane zooming by.

We found out later that a guy in a hut across the road from us had been hit right in the chest and killed instantly. An American soldier. A prisoner of war. By a stray bullet that came right through the wooden side of the building. He was sitting right on a stool, and it hit him right in the chest and killed him.

Those were really the highlights or lowlights of our stay at Stalag IV- B.

LIBERATED

The Russians were approaching from the east; the Americans and the British were approaching from the west. It seemed like only a matter of time before the war was going to come with the Germans still in between. And we were German captives in a German prison camp. We didn't know whether we'd get in the middle of a fire fight between the Germans and the Russians or the Germans and the Americans or accidentally between the Americans and the Russians. It was kind of worrisome at any rate.

The next thing (I know from my notes it was the afternoon of April 22), I was walking near the fence where the guards all had their bunks. They were all lined up in perfect formation in their best uniforms being inspected by their officers, and I thought, "What the heck is this all about? In the middle of all this, they have their packs, steel helmets on their heads, and what are they going to do?" I knew the Russians were coming, and there were rumors about what the Germans were going to do about it.

But the next morning we got up as usual, and that was April 23. We were rousted up by this British sergeant pounding with his wood stick on the side of the bed as we went down the row to go outside and be counted by the Germans. The appel, the British called it, meaning morning or something or wake up. So we all stumbled out as usual, and we discovered there weren't any German guards there.

Where were the German guards? There were none, we finally realized. They were gone. And there we were, left to our own devices in the barracks with nothing to eat that we knew of.

We discovered they had all left the night before. That's what I was watching the day before: a German-type inspection before they were going to retreat. They didn't want to be captured by the Russians who were at their doorstep.

I went over to the main gate, and I discovered that it was open. Someone had already opened the gate, so I stepped out to the main gate of the camp itself, and a number of others all gravitated to us, and there was a dozen or so men standing outside. I joined them, and it was a thrilling moment.

I thought to myself, "I am no longer a prisoner of war. At least not of the Germans." I didn't know what was going to happen next. And I realized how lucky I had been to survive all this time and not killed or wounded in combat or dead from some disease in the camp. That had happened to a number of the men.

I remember I didn't have to think what would happen next, because I looked up to the east and north and there was a caravan coming along. An all horse-drawn caravan. And I realized this was a Russian supply caravan. They were heading in the direction of Berlin. As I watched them in awe, thinking this doesn't look like much of an army, it was just like farm trucks filled with supplies.

As I watched I saw four men on horseback leaving the big caravan and heading straight for our front gate. They galloped up and I was just dumbstruck because they all looked so foreign. They all looked like cossacks. They all had mustaches and padded jackets and tommy guns slung over their shoulders. When they came up close, they reined their horses to a trot. They simply trotted past us, the two dozen of us, standing outside the doorway.

They knew exactly where the gate was, and they trotted inside the gate without even giving us a look or a hello or anything. We didn't do anything either. We were just awestruck, you know, west meets east, and we wondered what they were going to do when they got to the camp. Just the four of them.

It was a matter of some minutes, when I saw a whole bunch of Russian prisoners of war with fear in their faces running for their lives for the front gate. They were running out the gate, and they all looked very scared. I looked down the fence and there were more Russians arriving. The prisoners were tearing at the barbed wire fence, not realizing that a hundred feet away was an open gate they could have gone through, but they were terrified about getting out of there and going east.

I found out later that those horsemen had come right though the compound to where the Russians were camped and gave them orders to get out of the camp immediately and go east some number of miles wherever it would be or they would be shot. Something to that effect. They were considered persona non grata by the Russian Army now because the feeling of the Russians was that to surrender was to be a coward and you don't belong in Russian society again. These men kind of knew it.

Some of these men actually from this particular camp had joined some British group and formed a roughly small unit of formerly Russian soldiers who had been captured and turned into a brigade of a couple of thousand members or so fighting alongside the Germans against the Russians. And the Russians wanted them real bad, especially whoever had survived, plus any civilians or military people who had somehow fallen into the hands of the Allies, whether on purpose or being captured I don't know. It was a very strange sight to see the horsemen rushing into the camp, and then the men rushing out of the camp pell mell. Hundreds and hundreds. And I just walked away back to my own barracks. I had enough of that and trying to figure out what I was going to scrounge for breakfast or something. And pretty soon there wasn't a Russian left in the camp.

So they ran, to what, to where, I don't know, but they were all very panic stricken and scared. So I went back to the barracks and told the British what I had seen, and the British had been out there and everybody talked about how the Russians were here.

Then I remember that the gates were open and some of the men ventured out into the nearby farms looking for food and all. I remember one group came back, and they said they went into a farm house and found that a German couple had hung themselves. Their bodies were hanging by rope inside their house. They realized that the Russians were not going to be very kind to them when they got there. It was really sad to think that this was happening to them.

Then a few days later, I happened to be in what was really a jail inside the prison camp, a concrete block building in which prisoners were put for punishment for doing something that the Germans didn't like. They'd lock them up for a few days or a week. It was empty, and I had never been inside of it. About a dozen German soldiers looking very disheveled and dirty were coming in and being led to that jail by the Russians.

When I looked at them, I thought that must have been how we looked arriving at this camp. Dirty and disheveled, and these guys had been captured somewhere in the vicinity, and the Russians locked them up in jail. I went on my way, and that's the last I saw of them. I don't know what became of them. They seemed like ordinary German soldiers. They weren't high-ranking officers, just combat soldiers captured somehow in the vicinity. Life went on as we knew it, but with Russian soldiers all over the camp.

The Russians took over, and the Russians were amiable and okay, farm boys like many of us. Just doing their duty. Many of them had been in the army for five or six years. The Russians were feeling great. The enemy was about to be defeated for good.

It wasn't known to us at the time, but the Russian High Command and the American and British High Commands had held a series of meetings on how they are going to carve up Germany and so forth at Yalta. Finally thirty or forty miles away from where this prison camp was, the Allies and the Russians had met and made their final determination that the Americans were going to stop their assault eastward at the Mulde River, and thirty miles west was the Elbe River, also a north-south river, and it was agreed that the Russians would not go in strength beyond that point, and we would not go in strength beyond the Mulde River. A buffer zone was fixed between the two so that the two armies wouldn't think the other side was German and have a terrible, catastrophic clash. So that was the way they worked it out. It was thirty miles between me and the American lines.

After a week or two of decent treatment by the Russians—-they were busy celebrating the virtual end of the war, and they were happy to see us and all—-the British guys who were in charge of the camp informed us we were all moving by a one-day's walk from the prison camp to cross over the Mulde River.

We were given a pack of cigarettes and a piece of candy by the Russians and lined up to walk a day's walk to a new location. It turned out to be the city of Riesa. So we all walked along and took it easy. It wasn't that difficult a walk; it wasn't like marching.

We finally got to the camp and, lo and behold, they brought us to an abandoned German army engineering school. A two-story brick building and a place for eating. Of course it was all empty of Germans. They all assigned us to beds in these bedrooms and Larkin Mayfield and I find ourselves in a nice bed with like five to a room in nice army cots that were far better than the hard wooden table that Mayfield and I had been sleeping on for like a month. So this was just wonderful to sleep on a real mattress. They started to feed us, and all it was lousy food—-it was like peas every other day. I had a big case of indigestion, and I talked about sneaking out of this camp and foraging for food in the town of Riesa, trying to find something digestible.

We did it and several other guys were with us. We went into the town of Riesa and we come upon a Russian soldier on a bicycle. He seemed friendly enough so we waved to him and he stopped, so in sign language we pointed out that we were looking for food. We pointed to our mouths and all that. He smiled and waved and said in effect, come with me, and he took us to a very nice house. We walked in the door and we found two ladies. One of the ladies was holding a little infant.

The Russian ignored them and he went straight to the basement. He obviously had been there before, he knew the whole layout. He brought us over to this big, big carton of evaporated milk. We hadn't had any milk for months, except powdered milk every once in a while from the Red Cross parcels.

As we were thinking about filling our pockets with all the milk we could take, the lady with the baby came running down the stairs and crying and shouting in German, "It's food for my baby! It's food for my baby!"

She was very shocked and upset that we were going to clean her out of all the milk that somehow she had stashed away there. How she got such an enormous supply, I don't know. I could see what was going on and I said, "Fellas, let's just take one can each and get out of here. Let the poor lady have the evaporated milk for her baby." They all agreed, and we took one can each and to her great relief we left. With a knife, we punctured the top of the can, and we went out and drank this heavenly fluid which was so enriching to us. We hadn't had anything like that in five or six months.

I felt a little bit of a saint, to not take all of the milk, and getting the other guys to agree. In another house, I found a small notebook and a pencil and I started to write notes and writing a daily log.

We started looking at houses for more food and all. We found nothing. Most of the houses were all abandoned. We looked in the kitchens and nothing was available that was edible. So we were back to our usual starvation level, Ha, Ha, and we realized that there wasn't going to be any food for us. The Germans, the civilians had taken all their food and run for their lives.

While we were at the engineering school, the Russians grabbed me one day and put me on guard duty at the main entrance. They handed me a weapon, a Russian rifle. They said don't let anybody in or out at the main gate. They had a jail attached to put problem soldiers in there. I went into the jail and looked around and figured out what was going on there, and I figured out that they weren't watching me too closely. I didn't want to do guard duty, so the first chance I got, I went out with the rifle and looked around and there were no Russians around at the moment so I put the rifle down and ran off. We all looked alike to the Russians. There was no way they could tell it was me.

They didn't know my name. Nothing. They had just grabbed a guy walking by. So I escaped from that duty from the Russian Army, and I got back to my room. I was sharing a room with four other guys. We each had an army cot to sleep on, which was luxurious considering Larkin Mayfield and I had been sharing a rustic handmade table with no mattress of any kind for months before we were liberated.

I got back to my room, and I got back to my cot there and there was a closet next to my bed. I looked around in the closet to see what was there, and on the top shelf I found a packet of written German letters. And there in the corner of the closet was a German rifle.

I picked it up and saw it was loaded. I sat in my bed and I held it and I was looking at it and I thought, "I better cock this thing and experience this German rifle." I got the idea, "Well I'll just see if this thing works." I didn't have the idea that this thing was loaded. I thought it was probably empty. "I think I'll just pull the trigger and see if it is in working order," I thought, but then I thought, "That's a big mistake." Then I opened up the trigger mechanism and found that it was fully loaded with bullets. If I had pulled that trigger, one of those bullets would have gone sailing through the walls of that place. Who knows where that bullet would have ended? Maybe it would have killed a couple of Americans before it lodged in a brick wall. So I thought, "Man was I stupid for thinking about pulling that trigger." I just put it back in the closet where I found it.

ESCAPE

I was already liberated from the Germans, and now I was a prisoner of the Russians.

They had a high fence all around this place and I just couldn't walk out the front door. Like when I was a guard for a moment. I was supposed to make sure no Americans would walk out the door. There were one or two thousand Americans there. There was an airport nearby of one strip to land a plane, but it was all gone. It was evaporated. The soldiers who were training there were all gone, killed, or captured, or run away with their lives.

Anyway, we took over their barracks. We were comfortable. We all had our own army cots and we were being fed decently by the Russians. They would rustle up cattle from nearby farms, butcher them, and make soup. We'd have soup made of whatever animals they had.

We were no longer in front of the prison camp with barbed wire; we were in a place with a high fence all around it. A main gate and all that, and I discovered they also had a jail inside of it.

Well then after we were all settled in there, the Russians put an armed guard all around the outside of the camp so that none of us could escape from them. They had orders from their higher ups to hold on to us, all the prisoners they could get their hands on, until further directions from on high. They didn't know why we were being held, but their orders were to hold us there.

I was afraid I was going to end up pining in a Siberian salt mine or something. You never knew. Some did actually. We found out decades later that hundreds of my fellow American soldiers who were captured by the Russians were sent to their deaths in Siberia.

One day when we were there like a week or so, a convoy of American trucks came across the thirty-mile stretch of no man's land, with a few jeeps leading the way. They had heard that we were there, and they were going to load us all up on these two-by-two big trucks and bring us back in batches across the thirty-mile lines. The Russians said,

"No, no. Nothing doing. We're in charge here. You can't take them back." But they did bring along little canvas bags for each person, what they called a release kit. A little drawstring bag made of canvas about a foot high and half a foot wide filled with things like shaving cream, toothbrush, a razor, razor blades, a couple of packs of cigarettes, and things like that.

They had us all lined up in the field by this camp, and they handed to each one of us a release kit. Then we got to talking to one of the jeep drivers and, lo and behold, one of the guys in one of the jeeps was an International Red Cross representative assigned to my brother Bob's infantry division as the liaison. Let's say some soldier's parents died or were killed in a car crash or something, they would call on this Red Cross rep to call on the soldier to break the bad news and help him write a letter or do whatever would be possible to smooth out the problem, whatever it might be. Possibly ship him home by air, I don't know what would happen.

I said to this Red Cross rep,

"It said 69XX on your jeep," which meant 69th Infantry Division level and one X meant one division or regimental area, so this was XX, which meant they were from division headquarters. "My brother Robert, who last I heard was still in the United States, was in the 69th Division and maybe they've come over to here and maybe they are in the vicinity, and if my brother is still alive, I'd like to catch up with him."

The man listened with very great interest and took down my brother's social security number and his exact name and my name and social security number and so forth, and he said,

"I'll tell you what. They won't let us take you guys back, but they are going to let us take these empty trucks back. The Russians said because we ran out of these release kits, they are going to let us come back with one jeep and a trailer loaded with release kits, probably another fifty kits to give to the guys that didn't get one. If your brother is in the 69th Division, I'll have him with me when I come back in a couple of days with this trailer load of release kits."

It was fantastic news. Of course, I worried. I wondered if my brother had been killed or wounded or something or if he was still back in the states in a different outfit, I didn't know, nor did this Red Cross rep know. But as it turned out, this Red Cross rep went back and he told the commander of the regiment of which Bob was a part and told him what he had heard from me in the camp. The colonel in the regiment called for Bob to come into the office, and he told him the story, and the rep said he was going back in a couple of days, and he said to Bob, "You can come with me, if you want," and Bob said, "I'm going."

Anyway, Bob immediately got together a bunch of letters from home and some clean underwear and went by the bridge over the Mulde River. On the other side of that river was an armed squad or platoon of a large group of Russian soldiers, supposedly not letting any Germans escape from that no man's land and into American and

British hands. Well, Bob and that rep went to that bridge with a trailer full of Red Cross release kits, and they wouldn't let them come across. They said, "No, no." Our lieutenant said in pidgin English and German and all that their lieutenant said, "No we can't let anybody come across on the American side either." So Bob waited several days at the bridge.

Every day at the bridge, he got out there, and he had this package under his arm. Once in a while an American soldier would slip over the bridge when the Russians weren't looking, and it took them thirty miles and a couple of days to get there. Bob slipped across the bridge and he would say, "Do you know George Zak? Do you know George Zak?" Nobody ever heard of me. My brother Bob was getting frustrated.

And on my end. I was expecting them in a couple of days, but like a week and a half went by and nothing happened. I thought something had gotten awful bad that the Red Cross man with or without Bob didn't come back. So I decided that I was going to escape from the Russians in the dead of night and make my way across the thirty miles one way or another to find my brother if he was still there. At least find his outfit if it was still there.

So I told my good buddy, he was all excited about it. He wanted to come with me, and three other guys who were standing nearby heard me cooking up this story, and they decided they wanted to come along too. So there were five of us all together.

First of all, I reconnoitered the camp, the best way of getting out in the night with the ring of Russian soldiers with rifles turning back anybody trying to get away out. Some did and some got out. A few did get away, as the ones were crossing the bridge. The Russians were drunk half of the time and celebrating when they got a hold of any vodka or any alcohol of any kind from German stores and whatnot. I can't hardly blame 'em. A lot of them weren't doing their job the way they should have.

Anyway, I walked into a doorway, which turned out to be a garden. It had been used obviously when the German soldiers were there to grow fresh vegetables for them—-carrots, potatoes whatever. It had been a big thing, but it had gone fallow all winter and nothing was there except weeds. Just as I was about to open another door, on the other side of the door was a Russian patrolling along inside the camp. He looked at me, a friendly-enough-looking guy but serious. And he looked at me and he saw on my left wrist, a wrist watch. The Russians had never even seen wrist watches before. It was my cheap Westclox watch that I eventually gave to my son David as a present, which he long ago lost. I don't know whatever became of it. Anyway, I was determined to hold on to it. I had kept it from the Germans when I was searched because I was able to put it into a watch pocket. They never found it. And then I wore it, and I was using it like a compass some of the time.

This Russian saw the watch and with his right hand he reaches over and grabs my wrist on top of the watch and he says the English word "watch." He looked me in the eyes and sternly said, "Watch. Watch. Watch." He wanted me to give him my watch. I had figured out he was up to this game. This wasn't the first watch he was going to get off some nice GI.

I reached over and grabbed his hand. His tunic was rather loose fitting around the wrist. And he had watch, watch, watch, watch, watch—-he had about seven or eight watches already from other guys. I looked him in the eye and smiled, and he smiled back at me and let go of my wrist, and he let me keep my watch.

I thought to myself, he'll find a bunch of other nice GI guys who will give them their watches. He already had a half a dozen or more and he was just making his rounds, accosting anybody and demanding their watches. He was going to sell them for a lot of money one day in Russia, he figured, I suppose.

Anyway, I kept the watch. He went into the compound, and I went into the garden, and I thought this is the perfect place to escape to. It wasn't very far from our barracks. We could get there crawling from the basement of the barracks to that same gate. Open the gate up. Crawl through the garbage, trashy former garden to the wall and then stop.

We did exactly this at two o'clock in the morning. All gathered for the escape, the five of us, with me in the lead. I showed them the way, and they followed me. We crawled over to the wall, and then we stopped and I told them in advance,

"When we get to the wall, stop and listen for any sound of anybody talking or walking or gunfire before we attempt to go over the wall. We got to make sure that there is not a sound of any guard post accidentally or on purpose."

We did that. We huddled against the wall for, I don't know, however many minutes. Not a sound came from anywhere. We boosted the first guy up. He took a little look and whispered "Okay" and flipped over the wall. We flipped the next guy over. Finally, all five of us were over the wall. Then I arranged that we were going to make a big circle around the big camp building. Not go near the building for fear of running into the Russian soldiers, so instead of going due west, which is the way we wanted to go, we first went north. The equivalent of two blocks north or so in the pitch darkness and crept along without a word. Going further and further north until we were well past the camp itself and any Russians assigned to be watching us. Then we finally went west. Now we were south and west of the camp, and we had to cross over the field to get to the main road that would head west.

We knew where we wanted to go. Straight west. And that one road would take us thirty miles eventually to the American camp. We got to that one part of the road, and we discovered that there was a German infantry trench there across a big open field. It was apparently totally empty. Every German soldier had already left. It was an untenable position. But I realized that there could be mines planted out in front of that trench to blow up any attacking Russians coming.

By that time, there was another five guys we collected along the way in the darkness somewhere, so now there are about ten of us. I said,

"We have to cross across the field diagonally and across the trenches across the field to about a block away." I said, "Remember from our basic training? When we are going into a position like this walk single file and about ten yards apart, so if the first guy gets blown up by a mine, the next guys will change their route a little bit and miss that same mine group and hopefully the next guy won't be blown up and so on."

So in an instant, nine guys were standing behind me, ten yards apart. The fastest line ever right behind me. Yeah, I thought to myself, as a pretty smart guy, I'm the only one who remembered how to do this and now I'm in front. All these guys are behind me.

It doesn't pay to be smart sometimes.

I thought to myself, "I'll be blown up or have my legs blown up, but there is nothing else I can do." I thought to myself, "The infantry motto at that time was 'Follow Me.' Well I'm in the infantry and I know what I'm supposed to." So I said,

"Keep your distance, guys, and follow me." So we made our way across this way without a scratch. There wasn't a single explosion. If there were any mines, we missed 'em.

We got together about a block away. At the other end of this open field, there is this little dirt road, and along comes a Russian with an empty wagon with some milk cans in it and a horse that he got from a German farm somewhere. He was to be delivering milk in cans from the farm to wherever his soldier buddies were, I guess, and he was heading in the direction we wanted to go.

We put out a thumb like "Going your way?" And he stopped the wagon and let all ten of us hop on. Each of us gave him a couple of cigarettes. We finally got to a fork in the road where he wanted to go to the north, and we wanted to go west, so we each gave him a couple of more cigarettes, and he was happy to get them because cigarettes were very hard to get and they were as good as gold. We had gotten them from those relief parcels, a couple of packs each.

We each gave him two cigarettes, so he got the equivalent of like two packs of cigarettes for his trouble, and hopefully to keep his mouth shut and not to mention to anybody that he saw some "Russians" going by.

We made our way, and we were stopping to look at farms along the way. It was all empty. We were looking for some food. At one point we decided, the other three guys would go off by themselves. They were looking at some other buildings of some sort, and Larkin Mayfield and myself were walking together. Walking westward, and we passed this house and we decided to go back and take another look at that farmhouse to see if there was something to eat in there like an old loaf of bread or something. We turned around and went the other way, and who should be walking on that same street the way we had been walking but a German soldier with his rifle over his shoulder, walking toward what he hoped would be the American lines. The same that we were doing. We double-turned around backward to examine this house, and here's this guy with his rifle walking toward us, and we walking in his direction, and the German and the two of us decided not to make eye contact. We both pretended we didn't see the other party.

He didn't want to try to shoot us. He wanted to try to save his own neck by keeping out of trouble. We didn't have any arms. He could see that. Just two young American soldiers with no arms and he had a rifle. So it was one guy with a rifle against two unarmed guys. God Bless that soldier, that German soldier.

I don't think he ever got across the Mulde River like we eventually did, because he had to get past all those Russian guards. And I am sure they would have soon disarmed him and shipped him off for life as a prisoner of the Russians. I don't think he ever would have made it across. He could have made it to the bridge, and maybe into the arms of the Americans. The Americans would take him prisoner and he would be all right. He would be released, but not if the Russians caught him.

Most of the German prisoners were taken back to Russia to work until they died of malnutrition and starvation in most cases. Many of them were caught, not just there but in Stalingrad and Leningrad and the big battles there. Any Germans that were caught there, or any Russians for that part, were marched as much as a hundred miles to an uncertain future.

Anyway, we lost sight of the guy. We went to the farmhouse and found nothing. We did see a horse that was lying there dead with a big chunk taken out of his hind quarters by somebody with a knife. Somebody had probably shot the horse and taken a big part of his flank like his hip and probably roasted it and had a good meal for themselves and a bunch of guys. Who they were, Germans or Americans, I didn't know.

We found nothing to eat. Nothing at all, and we continued on our way. We got to the outskirts of a town called Oschatz, and just as we were approaching the town, up comes a civilian car with a British guy driving the car and he says, "You guys looking for a place to stay tonight?"

And we say, "Yeah," and he says, "Get in the car," and on the car it said with whitewash paint "USA" on the back of the trunk of this civilian car. A big, black car that he had found somewhere with gas in it, and he was driving it. It turned out he could speak German.

He drove us to a house in Oschatz, a very nice looking house. He says,

"You guys, wait in the car. I'll see if I can find a place for you to sleep for tonight." He knew we had roughly fifteen miles to go to get to the other side to the Mulde River to where the Mulde lines were.

He knocks hard on the door, and he's got an American officer's garrison cap on, but he had a British uniform on, and he spoke as definitely an Englishman. He got to the door with this American-looking officer's cap, and even though the Germans wouldn't know the difference between an officer and an enlisted man, it made him look more important.

He banged on the door, and a lady answered. She was a German lady and nice looking, thirty-ish, and he yelled at her in German and all that. He finally came back and says,

"Okay guys get out. I told her to give you supper and a place to sleep and breakfast in the morning and then you two guys will be on your way. So don't mess it up. They are scared to death and they'll take care of you without giving you any trouble."

So we did. We walked in, and they found some bread and whatever and they gave us some jelly and I don't remember what else. They pointed at a bedroom and there was a big feather bed in there we could share. There was an older man; I was nineteen years old and he looked to be an old man, about fifty years old at the most.

He was there, and I was there, and another older lady was there, and Larkin. Larkin and I both had some little supper and then Larkin wanted to go right to bed. He was exhausted. I was too, but this younger lady wanted some conversation, and she motioned for me to sit down there in a chair in the living room while Larkin disappeared in the bedroom, and the father and the other lady disappeared to wherever they were sleeping, and she starts telling me the

story of her life in German and some English and a lot of pantomime.

She said her parents and some other relatives were all killed
when the Allies bombed Dresden. She and possibly her sister or an
aunt or someone had come to live with this other old man who was
another relative, for a place to stay which was maybe thirty or forty
miles from Dresden. They were comfortable there but with a very
uncertain future.

She told me she was a "danseuse," as she said. She was a profes-
sional dancer, and she had toured all over Europe and even in South
America. Then she came back to Germany and the war came on and
there was no more dancing for her. She said her husband was a prisoner in Canada and a brother was in a Russian camp somewhere as
a prisoner. And I thought to myself, "He'll probably never be seen
again." But the guy who went to Canada, he would be well treated,
and when the war ended he'd go back to Germany.

We had a real nice chat and with pantomime and by that time I
had learned some basic German from hearing the German guards
yelling instruction to each other. What to do. What not to do. Get
up or sit down. March and so forth. Beyond that, basic conversation
bits. Between the two of us, we were able to figure out pretty well.
She was very good company, and I thought to myself, my, I haven't
seen a pleasant person, German or otherwise, for months. And here
I was having a really friendly conversation with a real nice-looking
woman, whose husband was in a prison camp.

She was very glad for some human company beyond the older
lady who lived there and the old man. We got along fine and later I
joined my buddy in the bed. I figured, "Well maybe during the night
they will stab us with a butcher knife or something, but I can't
worry about that now. I'm exhausted. I've gotta get some sleep." So
both of us slept soundly during the night. We woke up in the morning and the old man sliced some bread for us and put some jam on it
for breakfast.

Then we said goodbye to them, and we were on our way past Oschatz. We were walking down the road, and once in a while a German-made truck that was given to the Russians by lend-lease during the war, with Russian markings on it, went by on some task of some sort. They paid no attention to an occasional American straggler walking around by the road like we were.

And along comes a jeep with an American flag on the front, and there were two men in the jeep. We could tell that and as they came closer, we stopped to stare at them.

And they slowed down to look at us. And all of a sudden they put the brakes on, and at that point I recognized that Red Cross representative as the driver. I couldn't see who the passenger was because of the Red Cross guy's head in the way or whatever, but in a few seconds, I realized that that was my brother Bob. Sitting with this Red Cross rep in jeep in the middle of nowhere, really in the middle of this no man's land between the Russian lines and the American lines. Bob had gotten the word.

Backing up a bit, here's my brother's story: My brother Bob was drafted into the U.S. Army in 1943 into the 2nd Mechanized Calvary, which was a reconnaissance group that trained to go behind enemy lines and relay the information over the radio. Eighty percent of the soldiers in the 2nd Mechanized Calvary were killed in action. Bob was transferred into the 69th Infantry Division and sent to Rouen, France in 1945.

Bob's 69th Division headed toward the Ardennes forest right after I was in the terrible Battle of the Bulge and already a prisoner. Bob saw hundreds of dead American and German soldiers in the forest. He saw my 106th Division patch on dead American soldiers, and he realized that I could have been killed or a prisoner, but he knew I was close.

As German soldiers were surrendering all over, Bob's division settled in the town of Trebsen on the Mulde River. Our then–allies,

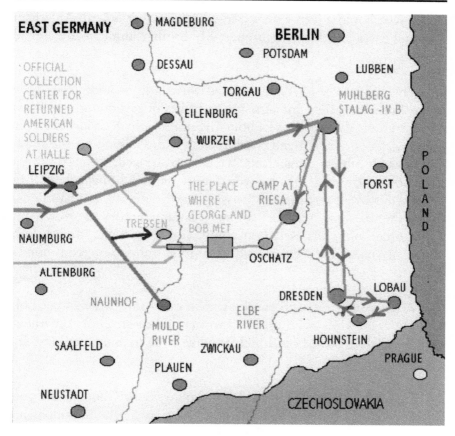

Schematic and map of Bob and George's travels through the end of the war. (Reproduced with permission of Peggy Zak.)

the Russian Army, settled nearby. The radio operators announced that the war was over. The Russians invited the American soldiers over for a party to celebrate the end of the war on the Russian side of the river.

An American Red Cross representative sent Bob a message that I was being held by the Russians near Riesa. The American Red Cross guy invited Bob to go with him across Russian lines to deliver toiletries and cigarettes to me and the Americans now imprisoned by the Russians. Bob's officer told him he could go, but he would be on his own with no reinforcements, just a fellow American soldier who spoke Russian in a jeep with a two-wheeler trailer and an American flag and extra cartons of cigarettes. My brother immediately agreed to go.

The Russian soldiers threatened them and wouldn't let them cross. But finally they got across with bribes of several more cartons of cigarettes. So Bob drove about five miles into Russian territory and saw me and my friend, Larkin Mayfield, walking on the road. This was absolutely miraculous. We were overjoyed. I was so skinny that Bob was afraid that he would hurt me if he hugged me. My buddy and I had escaped the Russian camp, but we still hadn't escaped the Russians. We were still on Russian territory but now with my brother Bob, the Red Cross guy, and a jeep and trailer. Bob shook my hand and he gave me some food and letters from home. We were very happy.

After we got through checking each other out, I remember Bob looking at me kind of funny, like I wonder if he's crazy or something or wounded. It turned out I had jaundice from malnutrition and my eyes were yellow.

I gave a big smile and said, "I'm okay, Bob. Good to see you and et cetera," and then he came up to me and we shook hands and put our arms around each other's shoulders, and I remember Larkin Mayfield was looking at us with jaw dropping that his own buddy had run into his own brother in the middle of nowhere, and the Red Cross man was beaming from ear to ear. Bob says,

"We gotta go on to where you escaped from to deliver these parcels, and then we'll come back and pick you up on the way back." He said, "Why don't you hide in the bushes there," and we did that. Bob gave me a box he had been holding with some clean underwear in it and a bunch of letters from home, and a couple of magazines, and some cigars and cigarettes, and stuff like that. I gave the cigars to my buddy Mayfield, who was a real smoke-a-holic, and I was reading all the letters from home.

I found out to my delight that my parents were very worried about me from what they wrote to Bob. Bob was also pretty much in danger because of the war, but he was never captured. He was shot at a number of times and whatnot, once a plane riddled the wall next to his truck.

We had a great reunion there, and we finally warmed up to the fact that neither one of us had a scratch on us that you could see, and we were still able to get around and walk and all, and we were okay except for me being skinny as a. . . . I don't know how many pounds I lost. I guessed from about 155 to 120 as a prisoner of war.

As we were waiting for Bob and the Red Cross rep to get back, along comes the other three guys. They finally caught up to us where we were, and we told them all about my brother stopping off and they were going to come back for us, so they joined us hiding in the shrubs waiting to get a ride home the last fifteen or ten miles whatever to the American lines.

So Bob got to Riesa and it was very clear that something terrible was happening. The Russians were formerly our allies, and now they were our enemies. The Cold War had just begun, and we were in the cross hairs of a new conflict. The Americans, after suffering being prisoners of war of the German Army, were now prisoners of the Russian Army and the Russians were very angry with him for coming and asking for information about Americans in Russian-held territory.

The Red Cross representative talked to the Russians in charge, and it was a very clear that the American GIs were prisoners of the Russians, and they were not going to let them go. Several GIs handed Bob letters, and then all of the GIs were hollering and tossing their letters to home at Bob's feet. Bob put all the envelopes that he could into the jeep. The Russian soldier put his rifle in Bob's face and motioned Bob out of the camp with his gun.

Then this Russian guy on a motorcycle raced toward Bob, spun out, and went flying. The Americans were cheering and laughing and this gave more American GIs the opportunity to get out of the gate. The Red Cross guy told Bob that he had better go pick me up before it was too late for all of us to escape. They drove out, leaving those poor souls. Of course they didn't know at the time what would become of them. Decades later, we learned the fate of those American soldiers imprisoned by the Russians: They were sent to Siberia and killed.

It was heartbreaking for Bob. The American soldiers were tossing him letters and yelling at him to call their loved ones. There was no way Bob could get any of them out. And all of those soldiers were killed by the Russians, I am sure. It was so sad. The Americans had fought the war and now were imprisoned again and killed.

Then Bob found about twenty-five American GIs who had just escaped from the camp waiting for him by the road. Bob and the Red Cross guy started a shuttle operation with the now ex-POWs. They would drive half a mile, turn around and get the rest of the guys, and they kept doing this shuttle all the way until they picked up me and Larkin again.

Bob looked big and healthy, and all of us were all wasted with poor nutrition and a variety of wounds and torn-up clothing and filthy. Bob ended up walking and then even carrying one American soldier who couldn't walk anymore because of wounds or exhaustion. All of the ex POWs helped each other walk for miles.

Bob was afraid that the Russians might send trouble after them, so they walked and shuttled as fast as they could. Now we had a big group of American soldiers walking toward the American lines. They saw American trucks driving toward them on the road, and Bob had them all hide. It turned out they were Russians stealing American trucks and driving them to the east. Bob was correctly afraid that the Russians would just stop and force all of them into one of the trucks and that would be the end of them.

Anyway we finally made our way to just a low spot in the ground with a hill in front of it just before the Mulde Bridge, and it was filled with a whole bunch of guys who had made their way on foot all the way from that same camp I had been at. Some dozens, I don't know how many there were. Could have been thirty or forty guys there, afraid to approach the bridge because they knew the Russians were grabbing anybody who tried to cross the bridge, and they didn't know what to do. The Red Cross man sized up the situation right away and he said,

"I'll tell you what. . . ." He took the flag off the front of his jeep and he handed it to one of the guys who looked like he knew what he was doing and he said,

"You hold this flag and everybody follow the guy with the flag and march toward the bridge, and we are going to go ahead with the jeep just in front of you. We'll run over anybody who tries to stop us. We will drive across the bridge and set the alarm that a bunch of American soldiers are at the bridge being held up by the Russians and have the Americans come to rescue us." That was the plan.

I was going to stay in the jeep in the passenger front seat, and the Red Cross rep was going to drive. Bob was in the back seat with some of the other soldiers, and we had the empty trailer filled with soldiers, as many as could fit in. So we started to make our way as grandly as we could make it. like a marching group who knew what they were doing, toward the bridge.

It turned out that there was nobody at the bridge at that moment. They were all off having lunch or something. We marched across the bridge with the American flag flying behind us behind our jeep and crossed the bridge into freedom's hands into the American lines.

I stayed with Bob for three days at the little town called Trebsen, where his unit was parked, at the Mulde River, but on the western side of the river. So we were safe and I stayed with him for days in a house they had taken over. They had taken the radio truck up against the kitchen window and ran all the cables into the house so they could send coded messages. Being in the kitchen while they were doing it meant they'd have a place to stretch their legs instead of being cramped in the back of a truck.

We spent hours there catching up on news from home. We'd had no news whatsoever. I had no idea whether my parents knew I was a prisoner of war or whether I was dead or not, and Bob had assured me that they had heard nothing except that I was a prisoner of war.

The Germans had tried to release the letters that I had written once a month, but they hadn't mailed them or at least had them held up by bad transportation. They finally arrived in Forest Park, I learned later, just about the time Bob and I were meeting. This would have been late April.

Being back in the U.S. Army was a very satisfying thing. I could hardly believe my good luck. Not only had everything broken my way, I apparently had made the right decisions along the way, such that I was able to survive the imprisonment itself as some others didn't and plenty got killed during the battle before that. The only down side was my health. I was not in good shape. I was as skinny as a rail and, standing next to my brother Bob, I know he looked strong and fit and I looked the same way myself five or six months before.

I know there was one picture taken of us together where Bob looks big and strong, and I look skinny and weak, and that was after about a month after I had been eating regular food again. So I had been much skinnier at the time when Bob and I met.

Bob and George at Halle

I want to mention that when we had gotten to the American Army, I decided that I was going to stay with my brother. It turned out that Bob's outfit was right there near the bridge. The headquarters was some miles back further to the west, but his signal outfit turned out to be a three-quarter-ton truck filled with radio equipment which he was in charge of.

By the time we had got there, they wanted to put us on these trucks to ship us to the town of Halle, where they were collecting prisoners, but I decided that I wanted to stay with Bob. So I said goodbye to Larkin Mayfield, and he got on the truck along with those other guys. I never saw Larkin again, although I did have a couple of Christmas cards from him and vice versa after the war. Then I lost track of him.

I stayed with Bob. Bob and I wrote a joint letter home to our mother and father assuring them that both of us were alive and well and safe and happy, and the war was over. I was very glad that we wrote that letter together, and Bob assured me it would be mailed in the regular Army section.

I think it was Bob, along with his supervising sergeant, who decided because of my health that I really should go on to the official collecting point. They would drive me there in a jeep. The next day I went to the regular mess (that's a cafeteria). I had breakfast there with eggs and stuff like that. Regular American bread. It was wonderful.

As we went to the collecting point, we passed through Leipzig. I spoke of Leipzig earlier, where they had asked for volunteers to go to this place to help dig out ruins from the bombing, and there would have been bodies to be moved and junk to be gathered up and all that kind of stuff, a pick-and-shovel kind of job.

I decided I didn't want to get involved in that, and I'd slipped away from the group, and here we were a few months later driving through Leipzig on the way to Halle, the collection city was Halle but Leipzig was a more famous town, and there was a big monument in the town. It was all pock-marked from shells from the American Army, but the shells didn't penetrate much because the walls were so thick. It was a military monument maybe built after World War I.

Bob told me that he was the signal guy in charge when they were relaying the artillery directions for shelling this building and other places in the town of Leipzig during the battles. Now it was all gone. All the German army guys were killed or all surrendered. We went on our way. I thought, "Wow, that was a good decision I made back when I didn't want to be in the middle when the American army came in." I didn't know what would have happened to me then. I could have been killed by mistake.

We finally arrived at Halle, and they had set up a very well-organized center for former prisoners of war. They had us fill out some forms and say who we were: our name, what outfit we had been in, where we had been captured.

They had organized a place for Recovered Allied Military Personnel. So we were now called RAMPs for short. They always had abbreviations. They treated us really well. They set up a nice mess hall in the buildings and assigned each of us to a cot and also allowed us each approval to give half of our standardized telegram to our folks back home to let them know I was okay and would be seeing them soon.

I had nothing to do with the wording of it. It was just a blanket form to just say I'm back in U.S. Army control, and I'm being well cared for, and I'm fine, and I'll be in touch with you soon again. So I very happily agreed to that. Later when I got home, I found out they had gotten such a telegram and were thrilled to have it, to know that I was now actually back in the U.S. Army and it was a joyful time.

I was overcome with joy with the whole situation.

AFTER WAR AND COURTSHIP

After the war, I got my degree in psychology from Loyola University because I really wanted to help my fellow man after seeing all that suffering and tragedy in the war. I ended up working in the personnel department of Western Electric Company in Chicago. Western Electric was a huge manufacturing plant that made all the phones and cables.

I had dated many a girl in my college days and none of them had been that super to me. I'd been on a lot of goofy encounters with young ladies, none of which really suited me. I thought maybe I'm a nerd and I'll be single all my life.

One day at college a female student pushed me into the school darkroom and shut the door and turned off the lights. I quickly flipped the lights back on. The lady told me,

"If I had an atomic bomb, I'd throw it at you." I wasn't worried because I knew she didn't have one.

I thought about whether I wanted to get serious with this girl or that girl, and the answer was always no. I thought part of it might

123

Joan as a young woman

be me. Maybe I'm just a nerd. Then I met Joan when we were working at the Western Electric Company in Chicago.

We had never met before, and we found ourselves walking together with a group of employees exiting the building to get on the bus after work. She worked on the third floor in the law department. I worked on the first floor in the employment department.

In short order I find myself walking alongside this beautiful young lady, all dressed for winter, and I caught a glimpse of her face, and I thought what an angelic and beautiful and charming-looking lady. We got talking a little bit and then I didn't know if she was married, single, or engaged, but I did know that I found her sweet looks very becoming and attractive to me.

I thought to myself, "That's a pretty lady. I wonder what she is like." I knew in short order that she was educated, she was smart, and she had very nice manners. We finally got to the bus. I didn't even know her name yet. She sat in one of the few remaining seats. I thought this is a lady that I would like to know better, and I wondered if she would actually respond to an overture from me.

I saw her sitting there right near the bus driver, and I walked right by her and tried to smile at her, and I walked over to where she was sitting. I grabbed the bus strap hanging from the ceiling I stood over her all the way to my stop. During that stop I discovered that she was single and that her name was Joan—all by clever questions on my part. I didn't say, "Are you single?" You get around that in other ways. I discovered this in a short twenty-minute ride. I knew she was beautiful. Smart. She responded to me with a very friendly, interested attitude. I thought, "Wow. Why isn't this girl taken?" She had to get off first to transfer to another bus to go further north to where she lived, roughly, Sayre Avenue and Harlem.

I thought about her all the time. I finally got the nerve to go into a private office that wasn't mine to ask Joan out on a date and ask her to lunch at a corner restaurant nearby. To my delight she said,

"That would be fun. I'd love to go out to lunch with you." We had a real nice time at the restaurant, and we immediately made plans to have plans for lunch every day.

Joan was attracted to me, and I don't know if you can say that early in the relationship that you are in love, but we were certainly thrilled to be in each other's company. That was the beginning of endless romance. We just never looked for anybody else. We just loved each other from the beginning.

I learned a lot more about Joan over the lunch and vice versa, and I had a very wonderful time and I went home with a just a song in my heart. What a lovely lady. She didn't seem to dismiss me. Joan seemed to like me. I think we had it worked out we'd go to lunch with each other and we did and all the while I thought, "This is the girl for me."

Our first real date, of all things, was ice skating in Columbus Park, Chicago. It turned out that Joan loved to ice skate. It was unusual thing for a first date. We had a wonderful time at Columbus Park where there was a big flooded area where you could skate. Arm in arm making circles. Joan could skate pretty good.

It was a wonderful beginning for us. She was just the perfect fit for me, and I was the perfect fit for her. The more we learned about each other, the more we were sure "This is the girl for me, this is the guy for me."

We had many of happy dates of all kinds. We did all kinds of theater, movie, the symphony concerts, parties and even an airplane ride. It just turned out to be a wonderful beginning of what would be a forty-eight-year marriage full of love and happiness.

Joan's mother told me much later, after we were engaged, Joan's side of the story about her meeting me. Joan's mother said that when Joan got home she told her mother, "I met the nicest young man on the bus today and I think he's going to call me," and of course I did and the rest is history.

Anyway, we had a wonderful life together and courtship and it was wonderful except that her father was against it. I wasn't the wrong religion. I was the wrong ethnic background. She came from an Irish family and I came from a Bohemian family. Joan told me early on,

"My father is very unhappy with you. He knows I've been having dates with you. He's an Irishman." Joan's father finished, I think, eighth grade and then he went to work. He came from a poor background. Mr. McAndrew worked on the railroad tracks for Union Pacific all his life. He left for work at noon and returned after nine o'clock at night six days a week. So Mrs. McAndrew did all of the cooking and raising of their seven children. On Sundays, he would sit and smoke cigars all day.

Joan's mother had a high school education and a business degree, which was quite unusual at that time. She also was precinct captain for their district in Chicago and played the organ for many churches around town.

Joan told me her father's idea of what a young Irish girl should do about her life. The best thing she could do would become a nun. Joan's older sister did that. The very next best thing she could do would be to marry a nice Irish boy. And third would be to not marry and stay home and take care of the house with her mother. And I didn't fit into any of those categories, because I had a Bohemian heritage.

I would take Joan home, and we used to sit in the car for like fifteen minutes chatting about the day. When Joan got out of the car, he was waiting for her inside.

"You've been out with that guy again. I know."

That was the worst of that.

Joan's brother, Harold, was also a prisoner of war during World War II. He was captured by the Japanese in the Philippines on Bataan. He was treated savagely and died of starvation and disease five months later during the Bataan Death March. Joan and her entire family were terribly shaken up by Harold's death under horrific conditions. He starved to death after being abused physically. It was awful. After the war, the United States recovered and sent home six pounds of bones to Joan's parents to bury—all that was left of Harold.

A fellow soldier who was imprisoned with Harold was with Harold when he died. The two of them were sitting up against a wall somewhere, and poor Harold was obviously dying. The other

PFC Harold McAndrew in the Philippines

soldier couldn't help Harold in any way and finally Harold stopped breathing. This other man somehow survived and was eventually repatriated to the United States. The whole McAndrew family went through terrible, terrible times over the loss of their son. They didn't know what happened to Harold for over a year. Every Sunday during the war, Mrs. McAndrew and the mothers of the other missing soldiers stood on the Michigan Avenue bridge holding bouquets of flowers in honor of their sons. So sad.

The McAndrews also dutifully attended the Maywood Bataan Society to discuss the possibility of their sons' returning, although of course most of them were already murdered but their families didn't know that at the time. Today the Maywood Bataan Society is still operational after over seventy years, still commemorating the suffering of the soldiers.

Esther McAndrew on Chicago's Michigan Avenue bridge. The mothers of missing soldiers met on the bridge every Sunday for years.

And at some point Joan had told her father about my being a prisoner of war by the Germans, and I think when she told her parents about how I was captured in battle, and how I was imprisoned and escaped from captivity, it kind of softened Joan's father a little bit and he took a different view of me.

Finally one day, when Joan and I were really in love and headed for engagement and marriage, I was invited over, and I wanted to ask his permission for Joan's hand in marriage. We were all set to set a date, we were going to pick out a ring, and he was being more civil to me.

That evening, he also had Joan's brother, Tom, the priest there with him. Both Joan's father and Tom were was very interested in my experience of being a prisoner of war. The two of them were sit-

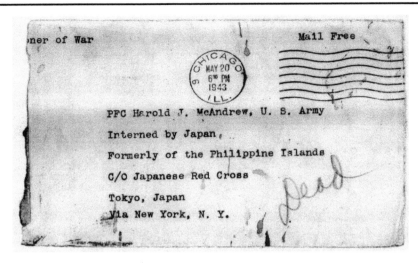

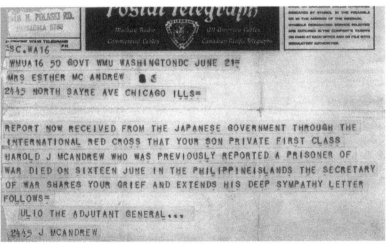

Official telegram notification of Harold's death

ting on the couch facing me, and I was sitting in a chair. They were questioning me, and I told them what it was like and that I was familiar with the experience that Harold went through. I said,

"I read books about it and my experience was terrible but his was much worse I have to tell you." And I think that was what finally made Joan's father decide I was all right.

Maybe there is a fourth category. A good Bohemian guy.

I finally knew. I won the battle with him.

Joan had to wait in the living room. Joan's father beckoned me into the kitchen, and he went into a walk in the pantry. He had a bottle of booze there, and two shot glasses, and he poured a glass for him and for me. We both had a drink together. So I guess I was a semi-Irishman after that. A potato eater.

It breaks me up, too, when I think about the tender moments in my life. It ended so happily when Joan accepted my invitation to marry. And I knew she would.

Joan and her mother went downtown to visit a cousin of hers who was in the jewelry business to pick out a wedding and engagement ring, which thrilled Joan and myself. Joan and her mother went downtown and picked out her wedding dress. The first dress she tried on was the one she bought. It was just perfect. And I've had a lot of compliments on that beautiful gown. Not long after, though, her mother suddenly died, and her father was sick that time himself. I was in my office and I knew that Joan's mother wasn't very well. I got a call from a priest from her parish and he said,

"Mrs. McAndrew is very ill and go get Joan and bring her home right away." I asked if she passed away and he wouldn't say. He just said bring her home right away.

Everybody had to have an identification card to show to the company guards that you really worked there, and her card had a special identification that she was allowed to come and go with a briefcase as a messenger. I sat in the car watching down the street, and I saw Joan sure enough walking with her briefcase and I said,

"Your mother is sick and I want to take you home." Joan was very silent because she knew her mother was ill and she

Joan and George's wedding portrait

didn't ask me if her mother had passed. I didn't know myself. I asked the priest, and he ignored my question. He said just come bring her home. When we got home to her home, we walked in the door.

Her father was there and he was sitting at the dining room table and he was all broken up and he was sick himself with problems that were bedeviling himself from time to time. And he waved at us like "Oh, oh, oh," and it turned out she was laid out in the bedroom. Joan took if very stoically. She was very broken up, but we

George and his daughter, Suzanne

stayed there and prayed some at her bedside. Joan was so sad and sorry that her mother wouldn't be at her wedding.

I have to agree that to me it's the most beautiful wedding dress you could have. Joan and her mother picked it out. [George points to their wedding picture.] And we lived happily together for forty-eight and a third years. Look what happened. Four fabulous children including our one daughter.

At our wedding, Joan's father said to us, "I wish you all the luck in the world."

FINAL MOMENTS WITH BOB AND GEORGE'S LEGACY

I have a very vivid recollection of Bob's last days and how we happened to be so close physically at the time he passed away. Bob had been ailing a lot at home. He was finally transferred to ManorCare of Hinsdale, where I had been in residence for some time trying to get over the problem with the muscles in my right leg.

I was astounded to hear that my brother Bob was being transferred to the same nursing home where I was living. Bob had been failing a long time. As far as I could see, Bob's mind was pretty active, but he succumbed finally to the effects of Alzheimer's disease.

I could see that Bob had failed a lot since I had last seen him. He had difficulty starting a sentence. You would ask him about something or other and he would start to talk and then his jaw would be moving, his lips would be moving, but he couldn't get the motor

135

started. He would get all mixed up. I was astounded and dismayed to see how he had deteriorated from the previous time before that. It was awful to see his decline.

Bob was a smart guy, he was a very practical and mechanical. Bob worked for a number of years as an electronics mechanic fixing up the radio and radar and so forth on a plane. When a plane would come in, they would radio ahead if they were having trouble with this or that feature of the mechanical systems, and it was Bob's job to go out to the plane in a little truck to do the repairs.

At ManorCare I would visit Bob every day and go over to the room he was in, not very far from my room, on the other side of the nursing station. Every morning, I would go there, sometimes he would be sleeping. He was there with a caregiver who would stay overnight with him, and I would sometimes get lucky and find that he was awake and have a little chance to be with him.

Bob really wanted to sleep all the time, but I had the privilege of seeing him every day for a number of days. It was wonderful to be together in his declining days, and I appreciate it. I'd get over there a couple of times a day, and sometimes I'd even had a chance to talk with him when he was alert and not sleeping.

I could see he was failing and so could everybody else and that was not going to go on forever. It really dismayed me, and I had such fond memories of Bob when we were growing up. He was my big brother, and I learned a lot from him about how to get along with other kids and all that and how to play softball and, of course, during the war.

I visited Bob sometimes even three times a day. My dear daughter came to visit and she brought along her guitar and a photograph album. She couldn't wait to see her Uncle Bob and try to get him to respond to her music on the guitar and the pictures. It was a wonderful time. I was sitting there watching my daughter pouring her heart out on her guitar.

Bob was starting to respond. He was listening to the music that my daughter was strumming on her guitar, and I thought that was so wonderful. I was so proud of that at such a time when Bob needed some stirring up to keep him going, and we had a wonderful couple of hours when she played the guitar and played various songs and was so wonderful.

Occasionally I would say something to Bob. It was a wonderful moment to see Bob getting back using all his physical and mental resources together again to respond as more lively every time than I had seen him sitting there every day. Bob was clapping, smiling, and having a nice time. And he sort of woke up.

The music must have awakened him. It sort of brought his physical powers back to where he was not just sleeping all the time. Bob was pretty much awake, and he was responding and happy, and my daughter showed her uncle the photo that rang the bell for memory. She showed him the picture that was famous, the picture of Bob and me together. This was about a month after we had met up in Germany, and I was already on the way of getting my strength and weight back a little bit, and I was happy and lively, and Bob was lively and one of the other soldiers took our picture, of the two of us together. Skinny me having lost about forty pounds in five months or so, and Bob looking hale and hearty, and he looked like I had looked when I went into combat.

There we were smiling and happy that we had met together and when he saw that picture, he sat up more in bed pointed at it and pointed at himself in the picture and said, "Wow!"

I was stunned with joy and amazed that that brought him back to when he was a soldier in the army again, and then he turned his view to my picture alongside of him and he pointed again and he said, "Wow." It was so thrilling and wonderful to connect to him again with me and us in our final days as soldiers in the war. And to me, as I recall, those were the last words I heard Bob speak.

Wow and Wow.

Bob looked at me and he knew who I was. It was clear to me. And he knew who he was. And I was so thrilled to be back with Bob in the days when we were both in the war and found each other.

It was a beautiful moment that he connected, he knew who my daughter was, he clearly looked at her and he seemed content and happy. If somebody had taken my picture at that moment, they would have seen the joy on my face at what was happening to Bob before my very eyes.

We were both smiling. And I said, "That's right Bob. That was us." It was a very gentle and beautiful moment. Bob had had that picture on this fireplace his whole life. He knew it when he saw it. He connected through the fog. It meant a lot to the both of us.

He found me and I found him at the point where we were both safe and survived the war. It was really unbelievable.

It was a joy to me to see that happen, and later the same day, Bob's wife, Peggy, came and saw me again. She was very calm and sweet as she always was, and we reviewed a little bit of when my daughter was there and I was there and Bob was there, and it was one of the highlights of Bob's passing for me. It really put a beautiful ending to the whole story.

You could see he was all worn out, trying as hard as anybody could to stay alive, but it was coming over him gradually. It was so sad to see him in the last stages, and it was merciful that he finally breathed his last breath. It was merciful, but it was also a beautiful thing that us two brothers connected. Clearly.

Bob had that picture on the mantle his whole life. He revered it. And took great satisfaction that he took part in finding his brother whisking me off to safety finally. That was a great story and a wonderful ending moment in his own life. And finally the wonderful end of it all from my point of view when she showed him the picture of our war photo and got a wonderful response from Bob and from me.

To think that that picture meant so much to both of us. It the most wonderful last experience he had conscious in his own life before he passed away.

EPILOGUE

Thinking about all my experiences in the war much later, I thought that the German people had brought it upon themselves, by falling in love with Hitler and doing anything he wanted to anyone else, including the Jews, to end up with a perfect Aryan race. They ended up with what they sowed. These people were typical civilians. The citizenry as a whole embraced the idea of being a super race. But they paid bitterly for what they sowed. The lady and her family that I stayed with in Oschatz was a microcosm of what they sowed. And her husband and her brother. I felt sorrow for them but at the same time, I felt they had brought it on themselves——not each individual person but the Germans as a whole. Then of course Hitler turned the screws and everybody had to do what he wanted and it went on and on that way.

I did feel bad about that. Very bad. I didn't feel that the individual German citizens were necessarily criminals. They just were duped into buying this master race idea and all that followed was nothing they could do anything about. Their sons went to war and many of them died and that's the way it was. They did pay a terrible price for their sins, for embracing Hitler's monstrosity of an idea of how to run a country. He wanted to conquer eventually all of Europe and turn everybody into slaves for the Germans.

I don't know if I can say what they did was evil. The Germans were stupid, maybe, to take advantage of Hitler's idea of being a super race and it was very, very bad. I don't feel I have to forgive them. They took a terrible beating in the war, like the lady and her family in Oschatz. Her parents dead, and her brother in Russia as a prisoner, and her husband in Canada as a prisoner. The one in Canada probably did survive, but I bet the one in Russia was never heard from again. That's the way it was. I haven't got it in me to accuse them. So therefore I can't forgive them.

I think they did an awful thing embracing Hitler, but it could have happened elsewhere. It could have happened in America that some monster got ahold of the reins of government and turned the rest of us into so-called super people. I don't know. I don't have any bitterness or hatred in my heart for the Germans.

In fact, I got well acquainted with a former young German soldier. A buddy of mine, who was also a prisoner of war, spoke perfect German, and he got a hold of a book, and it was somehow connected with the former young German soldier, who survived the war and somehow came to the United States on some kind of scholarship and studied history and became a renowned historian back in Germany. He was like seventeen when he was drafted in the German army and survived being in a prison camp along with his parents. Somehow or other my buddy, one of a group of former prisoners of war from the Chicago area, and I got to talking, and he was somehow acquainted with a former young German soldier, and he said, "Maybe you should get in touch with him."

We met on the telephone. He was back in Germany and I was back here in the states. He turned out to be a nice, cultured gentleman and a well-known historian, and he offered some of his books in German. I said, "Well I can't read them." I was waiting for the English version to come out, but that never happened. He and his wife and I exchange Christmas cards every year, and once in while I get a phone call. He explained some things to me about my own wanderings in Germany. He was very good about that. He didn't have a mean bone in his body. He was a very nice man.

I was just built not to be an angry, vengeful man. That's just my DNA. I have no love for the Nazis. I didn't run into too many of them. They were the ones that bought hook, line, and sinker the whole idea that they were the master race. And they were almost inhuman, the way that they killed millions of Jews because they weren't Aryran. Those people, I can only hate them as a concept but I can't hate them personally. Who knows whatever happened to all those Germans killed in battle. I didn't hate the German people. I hated the excesses of the leaders. They were monsters. I could never forgive them. It's not for me to decide who should be forgiven or not. I was trying to get on with my own life by them. I wasn't hooked on all the awful things that the Germans did to the rest of the world. I didn't think of it at the time, but I didn't let it become something that I had to carry on my back for the rest of my life.

But overall I know my life has been very, very blessed in so many ways. I have no complaints, nor should I.

Blessing from George

CPSIA information can be obtained
at www.ICGtesting.com
Printed in the USA
FFHW021702250319
51230868-56731FF

9 780938 075998